CONTEMPLATION
A Christian Path

CONTEMPLATION
A Christian Path

Willigis Jäger

Triumph™ Books
Liguori, Missouri

Contents

Preface

The desire to lay open deeper levels of consciousness is a general human phenomenon. We find evidence of it in the earliest cave drawings in Asia, Africa, and Australia. Without exception, each great world culture has developed a practical pathway into deeper experience—a pathway usually set forth within that culture's principal religious tradition.

In Western society today, more and more people are searching for precisely such a path. Having difficulty within their own faith tradition, they look outside the boundaries of organized religion, or to one of the ancient Eastern ways. In recent years, various schools of psychology and parapsychology have begun to address this age-old question. Recently, transpersonal psychology has also developed methods for penetrating more deeply into the human psyche.

Yet from its own earliest origins, Western culture, too, has been home to various esoteric paths. Within the Hebrew tradition, for example, the teachings of the Kabbalah have pointed the way into deeper experience. In the first centuries of Christendom, certain patristic writers began laying the groundwork for a mystical path within their own tradition. This contemplative path has at times flourished, at other times, been brutally repressed. It has always been an element of the Christian tradition. In the West today, Christians are rediscovering this contemplative way and walking it in greater and greater numbers.

Contemplative paths of various religious traditions are not, of course, the only paths into deeper experience. At times people have such experiences spontaneously, without any previous guidance or practice. Sometimes emotional shock, sexual orgasm, or childbirth triggers such experience. Others may come into deeper experience when coming out of depression or simply awakening from a dream.

Such experience in and of itself may be problematic for many. Without a context for such experience and the necessary help to integrate it into one's daily life, deeper levels of awareness may be more of a disturbance than anything else. Hence, it is crucial that such experience find a form of expression and integration. The Christian contemplative tradition, a reliable guide for leading people into deeper experience and for making it relevant in daily life, is one such expression.

In this book we trace the development of the Christian contemplative path as set forth in the writings of its principal teachers. We draw parallels between this path and similar paths in the East. Finally, we note in passing the ways modern psychology has shed light on various aspects of the contemplative journey.

Chapter 1

The Source and Goal of Religion

The mystical state is the highest level of religious experience and the goal of all religious life. It is also the goal of *all* human development, both on the individual level and in terms of human evolution.

The East has long recognized that mystical experience is the heart of religious life. But in the West, mysticism has not always been free to develop within the institutional Church. Accordingly, the mystical current has often flowed outside the boundaries of organized religion. Today, however, as increasing numbers of people seek a pathway into transmental experience, Western churches find themselves confronted with the question of mysticism in a new and urgent way.

To understand the mystical experience, one must understand the three levels of human consciousness. Toward this end, we can employ the terminology of Ken Wilber[1], who has systematized much of the ancient wisdom and the results of modern research in consciousness. What Wilber calls "transpersonal experience" coincides with what we refer to as "mystical experience"—without meaning to imply, however, that every transpersonal experience is a religious experience.

First, we identify the prerational, or prepersonal, level of consciousness. This is the level of the material body: sensation, perception, emotion, simple imagery, and symbols. This level may also encompass simple mythical conceptualizations.

Next is the rational, or personal, level, also called the ego level. This is the level of everyday consciousness, of reason and logical thought. The greatest achievement possible on this level is the integral personality, that is, the personality that has integrated its "shadow" with its "persona." This is the level of theological speculation, of grappling with the meaning of God.

Finally, there is the transrational, or transpersonal, level. This level is subdivided into three further levels: the subtle level, the causal level, and the level of pure consciousness.

The subtle, or psychic, level adjoins the personal level. Here we may encounter paranormal phenomena not readily accessible to most people. This is the level of visions, prophecy, and speaking in tongues. Since contemplation retains a pictorial nature, it is not yet formless. Although insights are still experienced within the context of certain structures and symbolic forms, the eye of contemplation is slowly being opened.

At the causal level, one experiences unity with a personal God—with Yahweh, the Father, Allah, Purusha, or Brahman.

The lover and the beloved are no longer separate. The Divine is grasped as an archetype of one's essential nature. One experiences oneself one with God, or even as God.

Finally, at the level of pure consciousness, referred to as "the void," "Godhead," "sunyata," "Tathagata," or simply "the ground," one experiences pure being. At this level, "pure being" is nothing other than that which emerges from it: "form is emptiness, emptiness is form." Nature and supernature are one. In Zen, this is the stage at which one returns to the marketplace. Consciousness is experienced as the essential process of the universe. All things are one, or rather, are not two. Jesus spoke from this level when he said "The Father and I are one" (John 10:30).

The basis of every religion is a revelation of the Divine to humanity, a revelation marked by two characteristics. First, it always occurs in pure consciousness, that eternal state of *philosophia perennis*—a form of theological reflection, metaphysical in nature, used in speculative theology—and is therefore formless, transverbal, and transritual. Second, while revelation always occurs on the highest level of human consciousness, it flows back into lower levels and there gains expression.

Diverse Expressions

For revelation to be expressed, it must take on the language and symbolism of a given culture. Thus, while the same Ultimate Reality is experienced at the summit of any religious path, the expressions of this experience will necessarily vary according to the differences in human cultures, tradition, and historical epochs. The Greek philosopher Parmenides, who lived in the fifth century before Christ, verbalized his experience in very different terms from those used by Plotinus in the third century A.D. or the Zen masters of the Tang dynasty or the

Indian sage Patanjali or the Upanishads or Meister Eckhart or John of the Cross.

If we truly believe in the humanity of Jesus, we must conclude that the foregoing was true of him as well: the cultural setting into which he was born and in which he taught determined how he expressed his experience. At different times, Jesus expressed his experience in very different ways—including the Lord's Prayer, the beatitudes, and his many parables. He referred to the Ultimate Reality as "Father," "Kingdom of God," and "Eternal Life." At the beginning of his public ministry, he declared, "Before Abraham was, I am" (John 8:58); in his farewell address to his disciples Jesus said that he and the Father are one. (See John 14.)

This variety may be compared to music. One "knows" a piece of music by hearing it. To be communicated visually, this piece must be written in a score. In turn, the same score can be recorded in various systems of notation, but the music remains fully identifiable.

So it is with experience and religious expression. Experience is comparable to music; religious language and symbolism correspond to the score. Religious ritual and practice are infinitely variable. They are never ends in themselves; rather they are only the means which lead into and express a direct experience of the Ultimate Reality. One must, finally, experience Reality for oneself; one must hear the music.

Interpreting Scripture

The words of Jesus can be understood on many different levels. Consider the conversation Jesus has with the Samaritan woman at the well. Jesus speaks about water—first about water from the well, then about water as a symbol of eternal life:

"...but those who drink of the water that I will give them will never be thirsty. The water that I will give will become in them a spring of water gushing up to eternal life" (John 4:14). The Samaritan woman, however, continues to "hear" Jesus refer to water in a literal sense: water from the well. She is puzzled and asks, "Sir, you have no bucket, and the well is deep. Where do you get that living water?" (John 4:11). Both Jesus and the woman continue speaking of water, but each refers to something very different.

Later in the conversation, Jesus tells the woman that God is not to be worshiped either on mountaintops or in temples, but in spirit and in truth: "God is spirit, and those who worship him must worship in spirit and truth" (John 4:24). Mystical writers understand this to refer to a form of prayer detached from consolations and sensory devotion. It is likely that most of them, like the Samaritan woman, fail to grasp the true meaning of Jesus' words.

Granted, it is comfortable to think of "the Father" as a kind of parental superego who rewards and punishes, blesses and condemns. Those who consider God a great father who watches over all, like a shepherd watching his sheep, will make petition the core of their spirituality. Their religious life will become an exchange of reverence and gratitude for God's protection and blessing. By living according to God's law, they hope to win for themselves the reward of eternal life. The "salvation" sought by this kind of religion is little more than a rescue from human suffering, evil, and death.

Eckhart says of such people that they are looking for something with God, using God as a candle with which to look; when they find what they are looking for, they throw the candle away. And again, "These people make a goat of God, feeding him on word-leaves."[2]

Elsewhere, Eckhart writes:

As long as you do works for the sake of heaven or God or eternal bliss, from without, you are at fault. It may pass muster, but it is not the best. Indeed, if a man thinks he will get more of God by meditation, by devotion, by ecstasies or by special infusion of grace than by the fireside or in the stable—that is nothing but taking God, wrapping a cloak around His head and shoving Him under a bench.[3]

When I pray for something, I do not pray; when I pray for nothing, I really pray....To pray for anything except God might be called idolatry or injustice. Right prayer is prayer in spirit and in truth. When I pray for some person such as Henry or Conrad, I pray least, but when I pray for no one in particular, I pray most of all. Really to pray, one must want nothing, for as far as God is concerned there is neither Henry nor Conrad. When one prays for what God is not, there is something wrong and faithless about the prayer and it is a sign of immaturity. As I said not long ago, when one puts something before God, he makes God nothing, and nothing, God.[4]

Such examples should not mislead us into contempt for verbal prayer. Eckhart was a priest and a monk who celebrated the Eucharist and prayed the Divine Office. As long as we are human, we will address and celebrate the Divine in word, image, ceremony, and ritual. Yet we need also be aware that these forms of worship are only "the finger that points to the moon."

The poet Angelus Silesius writes much the same thing:

> He who asks God for gifts
> is pitiable;
> he worships the creation
> and not the Creator.

The Divine as the Seeker

Any religion is bound by space and time. Its language, images, and concepts change. But the Divine is beyond space and time, giving no single religion property rights over truth. To really "know" the Divine, we have to transcend conceptual knowledge that is time and space bound. Even *thinking* of the Absolute is a limitation of it within the confines of the human mind.

Every religion agrees that the Ultimate Reality is inexpressible. "*Nada, nada, nada,*" writes John of the Cross: "Nothing, nothing, nothing." Eckhart says,

> Be silent and do not chatter about God, because by chattering about God you are lying and committing a sin....If I had a God I could understand, I would no longer consider him God!...You should love him as he is: a non-God, a non-spirit, a non-person, non-image, a sheer, limpid, pure One, detached from all duality.[5]

In *The Ascent of Mount Carmel,* John of the Cross writes of the harm done when one tries to define God in any way:

> Creatures, earthly or heavenly, and all distinct ideas and images, natural or supernatural...are incomparable and unproportioned to God's being.[6]

No form, figure, image, or idea that can be held by the memory is God or like to Him.[7]

Elsewhere John of the Cross calls all such images and concepts servants of the King. "The more attention he gives to the servants, the more he takes away from his lord."[8]

The great Indian poet Kabir addresses this same theme in many of his poems. Son of a Moslem mother, but raised by a Brahman, Kabir stood between Islam and Hinduism—both of which opposed his teaching while he lived (then fought over his body when he died). In one poem, Kabir gives voice to the Divine:

> Oh Servant, where do you seek me?
> See, I am already with you.
> I am not in the Kaaba nor the
>   Kailash,
> not in ritual nor ceremony,
> not in yoga nor in renunciation.
> If you are a true seeker
> you will find me immediately,
> meet me in the moment.

And the servant responds:

> Oh Sadhu—
> God is the breath of all breath!

The Islamic poet Rumi makes the same point in a poem about the drowning of "the fly spirit":

> The fly spirit fell into
> the barrel of sour milk of eternity.

Then there were no more
Muslims or Christians, Jews or
    Parsi.
Speaking of God is only
the fluttering of wings
that this fly spirit always does;
but if it falls in the sour milk,
no fluttering remains.

Ramakrishna once wrote, "All writings, every holy book, the Veden, Puranas, Tantras, and so forth, have in a certain sense been robbed of their purity in that they are but human expressions of what Brahman truly is. Brahman itself, however, remains untouched and unadulterated." Similar statements are common in the Upanishads, in Pantanjali, and in such Zen texts as the following by Daio Kokushi:

Oh my good worthy friends gathered here,
If you want to hear the thunderous voice
    of the Dharma,
Exhaust your words, empty your thoughts,
For then you may come to recognize
    this one essence.

All this points to the authentic mystical experience as an awakening of the Divine. John of the Cross says, "...our awakening is an awakening of God and our rising is God's rising."[9] Indeed, this is the story of all humanity—the story of our awakening, the opening of our eyes to God. It is the tale told by all religious books, a love story of the human and the Divine. And though we human beings may think we are the seekers, the reality is just the opposite. As the following parable suggests, it is we who are sought after and at last "found":

There lived in India an extremely rich nobleman with an only son who one day was kidnaped or lost. The father did all he could to find his son but all his efforts were in vain. Years passed without his discovering his child's whereabouts, and as the father grew older, his yearning for his son increased the more.

One day as the rich man looked out his upstairs window, a young beggar came to his house, was given something, and was about to leave the gate. The rich man saw the face of the beggar and jumped up in surprise, recognizing his missing son. Calling his servants he said, "Bring that young beggar here." His servants ran after the beggar and tried to bring him back. The young man refused to return, saying, "Forgive me please. I shall never come to your house again. Although I am a beggar, I have done nothing wrong." "No no, we aren't scolding you," the servants assured him. "Our master just wishes to see you." But they could not induce him to return. On the contrary, he got more afraid and began to tremble, saying, "I can have nothing to do with such a great nobleman." Finally the servants had to return and report their failure to the master.

The rich man, full of affection for his son, gave an order to one of his young servants to disguise himself as a beggar like his son and to befriend him. When this servant-beggar thought the time right, he said to the young beggar, the rich man's son, "I have found a good job. The work is not too hard, and the wages are good. They will also provide us with a small room. Why don't you come and try it with me?" Thus both of them were employed as gardeners to the rich man.

The son worked as a gardener for awhile. When he became accustomed to this position the rich man promoted him to house servant. When he did well in this work, the rich man put him in charge of all his property. Eventually the son was appointed his private secretary to stay close to him and manage all his affairs.

Years passed and the rich man grew elderly. Realizing that he would not live much longer, he gathered his relatives and friends together and introduced the young man saying, "This man is in fact my own son who disappeared when he was a young child." Then he handed over all his property and status to his son.[10]

This story is a good metaphor for the process by which we mature into higher levels of consciousness. It is always the Divine that leads us through these stages of development. Our task is simply to cooperate with the process by which we come to realize who we really are.

In the Old Testament, God is often presented as a jealous lover and humanity as the fickle beloved who continually runs away. The goal of this drama, however, is understood to be *unio*: loving union, a state of being also expressed by the word *covenant*: absolute friendship, unity. Moses proclaimed this unity of God and humanity to the Israelites, and it is this same "unio" that we must experience for ourselves today.

In the New Testament, Jesus is the side of God turned toward us. Through him, we may experience the side of God turned away, the side we cannot grasp intellectually. Christ is the doorway through which we can step into the divine space within ourselves. We call this step an awakening to Christ-consciousness. The Hindus refer to this as the Krishna-consciousness; Buddhists refer to it as the Buddha-mind or Buddha-nature. Jewish Kabbalists call this experience "return to the promised land"; Sufis call it "union with the beloved." Regardless of the name, this same Ultimate Reality lies within each human being. It is the goal of all these religious ways to awaken their followers to this fact.

Evolution and Original Sin

Eleven religions recognize the imperfection of the human condition. Many speak of a "fall from grace." But we may also view this "fall" as a step forward in human evolution, from a state of preconsciousness into a state of ego-consciousness. Awakening from the dullness of preconsciousness, men and women became aware of themselves as separate individuals. This was an important evolutionary step that took humanity beyond the level of instinct and unconsciousness, beyond the level of animals, onto a level that distinguishes good from evil, this from that.

With this awakening, however, humanity took on all the burdens associated with ego-consciousness: guilt, loneliness, an awareness of mortality and of the transience of all things. In the prepersonal paradise, Adam "walked with God": humanity did not experience itself as separate from the Ground of its being. With the rise of dualistic, ego-consciousness, however, humanity experienced itself as cut off from its Source, as placed in opposition to God and all things. This was humanity's "original sin."

Things might have happened differently. Humanity could have stepped into ego-consciousness without losing contact with its Ground. Certainly, there is nothing inherently "sinful" in this step, nor in ego-awareness as such. It is only when the

ego declares its independence from its Source, when one begins to think and act from this autonomous position, that sin
and guilt inevitably arise. Accordingly, our task is not to destroy the ego, but to bring it into balanced relation with the
Source from which it and all things arise.

The Genesis story relates how Adam and Eve discovered
that they were naked. This has nothing to do with clothing,
but suggests the isolation and vulnerability of ego-consciousness. The expulsion from the Garden is likewise an image of
stepping out from unconscious union with God into conscious
individuality.

The contemplative path is a path to experience directly the
union that original sin obscures. It is not a way back into Eden;
humanity has been barred forever from its previous unconscious
state. Contemplation has nothing to do with regressive desires
to return, as it were, to the womb. Evolution goes forward. We
are on the path to the New Jerusalem. Human consciousness
continues to unfold and expand in evermore inclusive ways.
Perhaps one day all people will understand that we have always
walked with God, that we have never, in fact, been separated.

Social Responsibility

People who take the contemplative path are often accused
of thinking only of themselves and neglecting wider concerns.
If this is in fact true of a person, he or she is not walking an
authentic contemplative path. The Christian tradition in particular has always insisted that one of the fruits of contemplation is a deepening—not a lessening—of concern for all beings. Eckhart writes,

No person in this life may reach the point at which he
can be excused from outward service. Even if he is given

to a life of contemplation, still he cannot refrain from going out and taking an active part in life. Even as a person who has nothing at all may still be generous for his will to give, another may have great wealth and not be generous because he gives nothing; so no man may have virtues without using them as time and occasion require. Thus, those who are given to the life of contemplation and avoid activities deceive themselves and are on the wrong track. I say that the contemplative person should indeed avoid even the thought of deeds to be done during the period of his contemplation, but afterwards he should get busy....[11]

A true mystical experience breaks through the barrier of ego and shatters any notions of self-sufficiency. Egotism, the fundamental burden of human consciousness, is cut away. Realizing the common life that pulses through all things, one begins to experience the joy and suffering of others as one's very own. And so it is that Eckhart writes,

If you love a hundred [dollars more in your own hand than in the hand of another, that is] wrong....If you love your father and mother and yourself more than another, that is wrong; if you love blessedness for yourself more than for another, that is wrong....There are many learned folk who cannot grasp this, and it seems hard to them, but it is not hard, it is quite easy.[12]

Elsewhere Eckhart uses the image of a human body in which each part serves not only itself but the whole: "The eye does not see more for itself than for the foot, but equally for itself and for every other part of the body."

Perhaps Eckhart's best presentation of this truth is his interpretation of the gospel story of Martha and Mary. It is not Mary, sitting in bliss at Jesus' feet, who is Eckhart's ideal contemplative, but Martha, at work.

One of the great misunderstandings of mysticism is the idea that ecstasy is the zenith of the mystical path. But ecstasy may or may not be part of a mystical experience. In fact, to be attached to ecstasy is to lose the experience of the Divine in every context—in every kind of activity and rest. Eckhart says that Mary had not yet reached this point, that she still had to "become Martha," to "learn to live."[13]

Mary and Martha, however, do not represent mutually exclusive aspects of being; contemplation and action are two aspects of one person. A spiritual path that does not recognize this, and lead back into everyday life, is not a true path. Compassion is the principal virtue in the esoteric pathway of each great religion. For example, in Buddhism, the most important vow recited daily in all Zen temples is "Living beings are numberless, I vow to save them."

Another Buddhist prayer reads, "In the moment of enlightenment, a boundless compassion arises within me. The more clearly I see this original countenance, the greater my compassion." The *Mumonkan* is a collection of koans compiled in China in the thirteenth century. The verse of Case 45 of the *Mumonkan* reads:

> Don't draw another's bow;
> Don't ride another's horse;
> Don't speak of another's faults;
> Don't try to know about another's
> affairs.[14]

In other words, when you draw a bow, it is always your own bow, even though it "belongs" to someone else. When you ride a horse, it is always your own horse. The verse also suggests that anytime we speak negatively of another, we speak badly of ourselves. It is this condition of boundless openness and inter-connection with all things that is the basis for compassion in Buddhism.

This same experience should be the basis for any code of ethics. Such a code will not be imposed from without, but the natural expression of the inner state of an enlightened person. Many of Jesus' words seem to point in this same direction; for instance, his admonition to love our enemies and his state-ment about our helping the least is helping him.

The true mystic is not a hermit looking contemptuously down upon "the world." Rather, he or she is one who grasps the divine in all aspects of reality. Eckhart writes:

> [Mysticism] is not to be learned by world-flight, by running away from things, turning solitary and going apart from the world. Rather, one must learn an inner solitude, wherever or with whomsoever he may be. He must learn to penetrate things and find God there....[15]

We are much more than our bodies and ego minds; the con-templative way leads us into an awareness of this reality, an experience of the transpersonal, a more inclusive awareness of being. Those who consider transpersonal experience to be irra-tional, even psychopathological, fail to see that in this more inclusive experience of being, we are likely to find lasting solu-tions to the urgent social and political problems confronting us today. This kind of transformation of consciousness has opened each new epoch of human history, and we are in desperate need of just such a transformation today.

Often our approach to social problems can be summed up by the motto of Europe's Young Christian Workers: "See, judge, act." Recognizing human suffering, considering its causes, and addressing these with courage and imagination: this is certainly a possible approach to social change. But the contemplative path, while concerned with human suffering, focuses in a different direction. The mystic knows that only an experience of the transpersonal allows one to realize the deep interconnectedness of all life. Such an experience transforms the human heart, allowing new ways of acting and being present in the world to emerge. In the contemplative view, personal transformation is a prerequisite for meaningful social transformation. Unless one awakens to the transpersonal dimension of being, even one's best intentions will be tinged with ego concerns that will tend to undermine one's work in the world. There is more than a little wisdom to the adage that "The road to hell is paved with good intentions."

The following story is a good presentation of the contemplative approach to human suffering and world change:

> There was once a village in China that had received no rain for many months. Its crops were failing, its animals dying, and its people on the verge of starvation. All of their prayers and petitions went unanswered: the heavens remained closed. At last, in desperation, the village sent for the great rain maker. When the rain maker came, he asked for a hut at the edge of the village and for bread and water for five days. Then he told the villagers to go home and go on with their daily lives at work in their houses and fields. On the morning of the fourth day, it

began to drizzle, and then the heavens opened at last and the rain came pouring down. The whole village came running out into the downpour and gathered before the rain maker's hut to thank him.

"How did you make it rain?" they asked in amazement. "I can't make it rain," he replied. "But it *is* raining," they insisted.

"Yes," the rain maker answered. "When I first came to your village I saw all the disorder in your fields, your houses, and your hearts. And so I went into this hut and put myself in order. Once I came into order, you came into order. Once you came into order, nature came into order. And once nature came into order— it rained."[16]

While not shrinking from decisive action, the contemplative refuses to act merely for the sake of acting. One's actions are, perhaps, less important in and of themselves than is the heart from which they arise. Only when one's heart is in order can the rest of society, nature, and all things fall into their proper place.

The Mystery of Transformation

The infinite shines forth from within the finite. Our individual finite forms are carriers of the Eternal. All religions teach that our individual existence between birth and death is only one phase of life, a span of time in which we grow and mature. In order to grow, we must be willing to continually let go of our present condition or state. For that which we cling to poisons us. If we hold onto food, for example, it does not nourish us or support our growth, but poisons us. Likewise with breath; we take in air and release it, giving our bodies life. Taking in and holding our breath will suffocate us. Taking in and letting go comprise the essential process of growth and development. Birth and death are analogous to inhalation and exhalation; each depends on and is as essential as the other.

The ego, of course, would like to secure its immortality, to hang on. But the individual form of any human existence is but one act within a larger play. Many acts precede it; many acts follow. This brief span of life is *not* the whole play—just as any personal death is not the final curtain.

The meaning of life lies in a realization of the immovable permanence that transcends our changing, individual existence. This permanence is the transcendent essence of humanity. Stability and continuity make up a dynamic that the mystic experiences as the current of all life. Such a person, living without fear, is open to the whole world. This state of being is expressed in the last of the Zen Ox Herding Pictures, which depicts the enlightened one returning to the marketplace. There he buys and sells, laughs and cries, and is not recognizable as a mystic—even to himself. He has forgotten his enlightenment and is living out of a transformed existence.

When we break through to the underlying current of life, we experience the eternal now. We begin to value life differently than we did before and, experiencing the innate perfection of all things, we are not driven to "change the world." At the same time, when any one person is reborn into essential being, the whole universe celebrates. If all men and women could achieve this state of consciousness, they could quite naturally live together in harmony. That is not to say without contention; individual human differences will always remain. But in this state of consciousness, humanity could live free of egotism. Ego-consciousness could at last take its proper place as but one state of human awareness.

The brief span of life between our individual birth and death is given so that we may accomplish this great task. This is never a question of mortification or annihilation, but only the falling away of all ego concerns; we need only surrender. Once we let go, we become the "guest of all things" rather than playing the part of the host. As such, we are not driven to "rule over" or "possess." We are content just to live, experiencing the current of life most vividly in simple things. The quality of our awareness, not the quantity of things that fill it up, becomes important to us.

This state of being, and the process by which we often come to it, is summed up in the following story:

At the edge of a forest lived a man who made a humble living chopping kindling and selling it to his neighbors. One day a hermit came out of the forest and the man asked him for some advice. "Go deeper into the woods," the hermit replied. And so the man did—and found wonderful, large trees he felled and sold as lumber. Having become wealthy, one day he remembered the advice of the hermit, "Go deeper into the woods." And so he went further on and came to a silver mine that he worked and became wealthier still. Then again, one day he remembered the hermit's advice and so went on even further into the woods. There he came upon a precious stone on the forest floor. He admired its brilliance, and remembered the advice of the hermit, "Go deeper into the forest." One day he found himself at the edge of the forest where he had long ago met the hermit. Happy as never before, he picked up his axe and began cutting kindling once again.

Religion as Obstacle

Religion, which should be one's path to God, can actually become a hindrance along this way. To use an image, religion might be compared to the moon, lighting the earth with the light it reflects from the sun. When the moon comes between the earth and the sun, however, the earth grows dark because the moon has no light of its own to offer. Divine life is like the sun: it illuminates religion so as to light the way for humanity. But when religion places itself between God and humanity, it eclipses the face of God. Eckhart warned of this danger:

> Again, good people are kept back from perfection by dwelling with holy pleasure on their images of the humanity of our Lord Jesus Christ. By the same token, they are hindered by laying stress on visions, in which they visualize the things of their souls, be they men or angels, or the humanity of our Lord Jesus Christ. They believe the messages they hear in spirit, especially when they hear that they are good people most beloved, or they hear about the faults of others or the virtues, or when they hear that God will do something they want done. They are often deceived, for God never does anything for the sake of any creature, but only for its pure good. This is the point of every Christian prayer: "Do this, O Lord, for the sake of thine only begotten son Jesus Christ!" Thus he said to his disciples: "It is expedient for you that I go away." …His humanity is a hindrance to them in the pleasure with which they depend on him.[17]

Elsewhere Eckhart writes that religious vows, too, may at some point stand in the way of one's path to God:

But if a man knows himself to be well trained in true inwardness, then let him boldly drop all outward disciplines, even those he is bound to and from which neither pope nor bishop can release him.[18]

For Eckhart, and for every mystic, the Ultimate Reality is not a personal God who rewards and punishes and helps the supplicant out of this dilemma or that. Eckhart views this kind of religion as part of the problem, not the solution. Again, this impulse to immortalize the ego, to set it up in opposition to some image of God and so to arrive in heaven with one's ego-consciousness intact, is nothing other than our original sin. Our salvation lies not in escaping this or that, but in the realization that God is the essence of all things, including suffering and death. It is this realization that is the goal of every authentic spiritual way.

The great responsibility of any religion is to point to the Eternal that lies at the core of temporal things. Few people are able to see this. Most of us try to find our happiness in temporal things: in work, financial security, relationships. Identifying with our bodies and our ego minds, we become frustrated again and again in our attempts to find lasting meaning or satisfaction in life. The primary and authentic function of religion is to point out the futility of all such striving and provide a valid way to achieve lasting union.

Karl Rahner observed that the Christian of the future will be a mystic or he will not exist at all. Humanity must grow into this new level of consciousness—or be destroyed by the inherent contradictions of the ego mind. The mystic—today the exception—must become the norm of human existence. The most important task of any religion is to do all it can to bring about this evolution.

Chapter 2

The Practice of Contemplative Prayer

The desert fathers were among the earliest teachers of the Christian contemplative way. In the first centuries of Christendom, these devoted men withdrew to the wilderness to live solitary lives of work and prayer. They called their simple form of prayer *ruminatio*. In ruminatio, or rumination, the monk constantly had prayer in his heart and on his lips. Saint Anthony of the Desert wrote in the fourth century:

> A camel needs but a small amount of food. It saves it until it comes to a stable, where it regurgitates it and chews it until it seeps into its flesh and bones. A horse,

on the other hand, needs a lot of food. It eats constantly and immediately loses what it has eaten. Therefore, let us not be like a horse, constantly reciting the word of God yet without embodying it. Let us follow the example of the camel, retaining every word of holy Scripture we recite until we have embodied it.

John Cassian wrote twenty-four Conferences as a help for persons who sought to pursue the life of the spirit. In his Conference Ten, Cassian guides monks in the practice of rumination:

> Our prayer for rescue in bad times and for protection against pride in good times should be founded upon this verse (Come to my help, O God; Lord, hurry to my rescue). The thought of this verse should be turning unceasingly in your heart. Never cease to recite it in whatever task or service or journey you find yourself. Think upon it as you sleep, as you eat, as you submit to the most basic demands of nature. This heartfelt thought will prove to be a formula of salvation for you....It will lead you...to that fiery urgency of prayer which is indescribable....Sleep should come upon you as you meditate on this verse until as a result of your habit of resorting to its words you get in the habit of repeating them even in your slumbers.
>
> This verse should be the first thing to occur to you when you wake up. It should precede all your thoughts as you keep vigil. It should take you over as you rise from your bed and go to kneel. After this it should accompany you in all your works and deeds. It should be at your side at all times. Following the precept of Moses,

you will think upon it "as you sit at home or walk along your way" (Deuteronomy 6:7), as you sleep or when you get up. You will write it upon the threshold and gateway of your mouth, you will place it on the walls of your house and in the inner sanctum of your heart. It will be a continuous prayer, an endless refrain when you bow down in prostration and when you rise up to do all the necessary things of life.

The soul must grab fiercely onto this formula so that after saying it over and over again, after meditating upon it without pause, it has the strength to reject and to refuse all the abundant riches of thought. Grasping the poverty of this little verse it will come all the more easily to that first of all the gospel beatitudes, "Blessed are the poor in spirit for theirs is the kingdom of heaven" (Matthew 5:3).[1]

These texts present the Christian contemplative path. This path is not only a way of prayer, it is a way of life. At the heart of this way of life is the simple prayer that Cassian, Saint Anthony, and numerous others teach. Unlike verbal prayer or meditation, each of which makes use of the senses, intellect, and emotions, contemplative prayer takes root beyond the level of sense perception and discursive thought. There is nothing wrong, of course, with these other forms of prayer; we are asked to love God with our whole heart, whole mind, and all our strength—that is, with all our being. But if we pray only with our intellect or will, we neglect something essential in our being. Contemporary psychology calls it the "transpersonal" level, that level at which we are able to enter into deeper communion with God.

We are all familiar with two levels of consciousness: the dream state and the waking state. When we dream, we are convinced that this alone is reality. When we awaken, we understand that there is a whole other level of awareness. Awakening onto the transpersonal level of consciousness is similar; we understand the limitations and distortions inherent in the functioning of our everyday minds.

Praying With the Senses

Sense and sound have the ability to extend our awareness beyond the limits of our ego boundaries. Allowing sense and sound to direct our attention inwardly, we can be led into a reality that extends beyond spatial dimensions.

I have always been deeply affected when I see people needing to make physical contact with religious objects of veneration. For example, when I see people in Latin America touch statues of saints or holy relics, I sense that it is much more than a magical gesture. In the gesture of touching their sacred items, these people seem to touch their own essential nature.

The mandala, a kind of emblem in the form of a ritual geometric diagram, works in a similar manner. It is a synthesis of a traditional structure plus free interpretation and is chiefly characterized by geometric shapes which are counterbalanced and concentric, each of which contain a way of seeing the world and oneself in transfiguration. The mandala, which occurs in many forms, serves as a means toward contemplation and leads one beyond looking to seeing, that is, into a unity in which the seer and that which is seen are not separate. One sees from the inside toward the outside until he or she sees from the outside to the inside, or rather until within and without are transcended.

Sound also has a dynamic power that goes far beyond its vibrations. Directed within it, sound can lead us into the depths of our consciousness.

Repetition

The use of repetition is a significant ingredient in contemplative prayer. It accompanies us to our death, indeed beyond death. Repeating a word or phrase is a form of surrender that allows us, in the hour of death, to let go of all images and pictures, to give ourselves over entirely to the will of God. With our prayer word on our lips, we die, delivered from the tensions of the world of form. We no longer pray to enter heaven, but that the will of God can be fulfilled in us: "Father, into your hands I commend my spirit" (Luke 23:46). This is not a deathbed remedy, but a guide for those to whom it has become a perpetual prayer through practice.

Although the West has almost forgotten the value of repetition in prayer, Eastern religions continue to highly appreciate it. In his book, *The Power of the Sacred Bond*, Blofield tells of an old monk who was asked about the serenity he seemed to radiate. The monk explained that it is the sound of the mantra, his repeated prayer, that allows the spirit, in a mysterious way, to experience its latent congruence with the Tao, the original path and the original meaning of being. Blofield writes:

> Finally I became able myself to experience the superiority of the mantric form of prayer. Because prayers have a conceptual meaning and that through them evoked thoughts are imposed on the silence of the spirit, the spirit can reach no peaceful and undisturbed condition in which the silence of the source is reflected. It remains attached to dualism: "I" the pray-er, "He" the worshipped. At its best, verbal prayer is a preamble to mystical union. And concerning prayer that contains petitions, nothing

could hardly be more unspiritual as to pray for victory or certain weather or happiness, which in the final analysis can only be reached at the expense of others.[2]

Many older people who have reached a mystical form of prayer with the rosary, neither knowing it nor making a fuss about it, realize what Blofield is saying.

Mantric Prayer

Most religions have sacred words and sounds that they constantly repeat, producing a sense of focus and concentration. Islam repeats the ninety-nine names for Allah on strings of beads. (It is said that only the camel knows Allah's one-hundredth name; that is, it cannot be grasped by the intellect, only experienced.) The Sufis of Islam have the Wazifas; the Hindus have mantras; the Buddhists use the *Nembutsu* or the sutras.

Christians, too, use the practice of repeating words as a form of prayer. The Jesus Prayer, for example, is a repeating of the same phrase: "Lord, Jesus Christ, Son of God, have mercy on me." The *kyrie*, "Christ have mercy," is also a repetitive prayer, as is alleluia, maranatha, and *shalom*. The rosary and the litany belong to the mantric forms of prayer as well.

The mantra captures equally the infinite and the finite. The infinite is experienced in sound, a sound that is neither a magical invocation nor a hypnotic tool. Rather, the mantric sound awakens power within us that is already present. The mantra connects us to something that is already there: it connects our ordinary consciousness with the depth of our being.

This depth of consciousness is more inclusive than language and concepts. The mantra, which is nonconceptual, is thus appropriate for leading us beyond language and concepts, away from ordinary consciousness and into a more inclusive experience. The meaning of the mantric word or sound is insignificant since it takes effect on the psychospiritual level, which is not subject to our discursive thinking. The mantra connects us to and reinforces ever-present powers and energies through repetitious prayer practice. It brings something in us into vibration. It channels us into an inner pathway and leads us to the wellspring of our being.

Tantric Buddhism says that the mantra "Om" is the most powerful; its power alone can secure enlightenment. Of the same mantra, the Upanishads say, "Whoever says this mantra thirty-five million times, the mantra of the sacred word, will be free of his *karma* and of all his sins. He will be released from all bonds and reach absolute freedom."[3]

In *The Way of the Pilgrim*, we read of the starets' instructions to repeat the Jesus Prayer twelve thousand times a day.[4] Whoever practices this for eight years arrives at a number similar to the Upanishad, that is 35,040,000. Repetition plays an important role in mantric prayer, for after a while, the prayer unfolds its own dynamic and prays itself.[5]

In mantric prayer, it is important that we do not create the sound, but rather that we become the instrument of sound. The sound should vibrate through the whole body. One can even address individual parts of the body, for example, legs, pelvis, chest, throat, arms, and head, and the mantric recitation and sound will loosen the physical tensions.

It is possible to charge the mantric sound with emotions such as love, trust, benevolence, and devotion. The mantra is also an effective means of releasing aggression, as long as the aggression is not directed against anyone. This is only an intermediate step, however. The point is to become one with the sound so that only tone remains. Everything else disappears, vanishing into the tone; there is only tone. Becoming one with the tone brings an opening of consciousness because everything vibrates to the same rhythm. Ego boundaries fall away, and we experience ourselves as one with the Divine in us and in everything.

The Rosary as Mantric Prayer

The rosary is the mantric prayer that is best known among Christians, especially Catholics. It has its greatest effect in group recitation, and the more monotonously and rhythmically it is led, the more dynamic are its effects.

My first prayer experiences are connected with the rosary. When I was about six years old, I participated in the rosary at church. It was led by a few women in the customary droning and monotonous manner, with mumbling continued by the parishioners. The combination of the droning and the mumbled responses would lead me into a condition of consciousness that was no longer ordinary. Even as a young child, I knew that a reality beyond ordinary reality stood behind the words. A litany could have similar effects on me; the singsong, repetitive sound could lead me into a deeper prayer experience.

Rhythm, droning, and monotony are necessary parts of mantric prayer. Unfortunately, this practice is easily misunderstood and dismissed by many Christians today, yet it can lead to a profound experience of the Divine. Something similar happens with the Jesus Prayer, which has a similar effect.

Practical Considerations

Your own way of prayer will emerge with time and dedication to the practice. At first, however, some practical considerations are worth reviewing.

A quiet place: Find a quiet place to sit, free from disturbances. Quiet has a soothing effect on the entire body.

An appropriate posture: Find a posture that allows you to sit comfortably for an extended period. This may be a chair or church pew or cushion on the floor. Sit upright, with your spine as erect as possible. Only when your back is reasonably straight can you sit in a relaxed manner and let your breath flow freely in and out.

An appropriate breathing pattern: Pay attention to the rhythm of your breathing. The Hesychasts, early Christian monks in the East, made "breath watching" the center point of their prayer. Rhythmic breathing stills your body and mind, an essential state to opening transmental levels of your psyche.

A short word or syllable: Many contemplative writers suggest connecting a short word or syllable to each exhalation. It seems as though words with the vowel "o" or "u" (*shalom*, for example) are particularly well suited to this practice. When you recite your prayer word silently, the last vowel will prolong itself naturally as the exhalation is extended. As you become comfortable with this rhythm, you will no longer pay attention to your breathing. Do not reflect on the meaning of the word; thinking and reflecting must cease, as all mystical writers insist. Simply "sound" the word silently, letting go of all feelings and thoughts.

Timing: A half hour is a good amount of time to devote to a single sitting. Because regular daily practice is essential for progressing along this way, it is good to schedule your practice at the same time each day. Eventually, as the patristic writers insist, this practice will not remain limited to your formal practice time, but will accompany you in every aspect of your daily routine. Your prayer will become a permanent part of yourself, continuing unceasingly and independent of your intellect and will. In time, it will even continue while you sleep and accompany you in your dreams. Only when this prayer permeates and encompasses all levels of your being may the Divine, which is within, be realized.

The author of the *The Cloud of Unknowing*, Meister Eckhart and Saint John of the Cross each describes the practice and the process of contemplative prayer. Each provides guidance for living an authentic contemplative life. Their major tenents are presented below.

The Cloud of Unknowing

A fourteenth-century English monk wrote two works that provide guidance for a contemplative life: *The Cloud of Unknowing* and its companion volume *The Book of Privy Counseling*. Both are written in clear, down-to-earth language by a mystic and spiritual director whose purpose it was to lead his student to a mystical experience. A close look at these two classics is a wise endeavor for anyone seeking the contemplative way.

Centering Your Attention

Much of our religious training emphasizes the use of our discursive thinking, imagination, and affective aspirations in prayer. While this is appropriate for meditation and other forms of prayer, we must abandon these modalities in contemplation. The author of *The Cloud of Unknowing* is keenly aware of this. A principal theme to which the author repeatedly returns is the transmental nature of contemplative prayer. He stresses:

It is wrong for a person who ought to be busy with the

contemplative work in the darkness of the *cloud of unknowing* to let ideas about God, his wonderful gifts, his kindness, or his works distract him from attentiveness to God himself. It is beside the point to say that they are good thoughts full of comfort and delight. They have, however, no place here![6]

I tell you that everything you dwell upon during this work becomes an obstacle to union with God....Yes, and with all due reverence, I go so far as to say that it is equally useless to think you can nourish your contemplative work by considering God's attributes, his kindness or his dignity; or by thinking about our Lady, the angels, or the saints; or about the joys of heaven, wonderful as these will be. I believe that this kind of activity is no longer of any use to you. Of course, it is laudable to reflect upon God's kindness and to love and praise him for it; yet it is far better to let your mind rest in the awareness of him in his naked existence and to love and praise him for what he is in himself.[7]

Don't be surprised if your thoughts seem holy and valuable for prayer. Probably you will find yourself thinking about the wonderful qualities of Jesus, his sweetness, his love, his graciousness, his mercy. But if you pay attention to these ideas, they will have gained what they wanted of you, and will go on chattering until they divert you even more to the thought of his passion. Then will come ideas about his great kindness, and if you keep listening they will be delighted. Soon you will be thinking about your sinful life and perhaps in this connection you will recall some place where you have lived in the past, until suddenly, before you know it, your mind is completely scattered.[8]

To keep your mind collected during prayer, the author of *The Cloud of Unknowing* suggests centering your attention on a short word, preferably a one-syllable word.

Choose a short word…fix it in your mind so that it will remain there come what may. This word will be your defense in conflict and in peace….Should some thought go on annoying you, demanding to know what you are doing, answer with this one word alone. If your mind begins to intellectualize over the meaning and connotations of this little word, remind yourself that its value lies in its simplicity. Do this and I assure you these thoughts will vanish. Why? Because you have refused to develop them with arguing.[9]

Elsewhere the author of *The Cloud of Unknowing* advises you not only to recite your word silently but to charge it with all your dedication, love, and trust in God. By placing all your longing in this word, you turn it into an act of generalized praise and petition without content or reflection. The word then becomes an all-embracing act of love that takes hold of your whole being, making it unnecessary to speak any other words before God:

Let this little word [God] represent to you God in all his fullness and nothing less than the fullness of God. Let nothing except God hold sway in your mind and heart.[10]

Don't be surprised if, after a while, your word becomes completely empty. It may lead into dryness and what the mystics call the desert, even into the "dark night." Fidelity to the practice is essential, regardless of your state of mind.

Forgetting Self

It has often been suggested that the contemplative path is a selfish pursuit, an egocentric turning away from others in favor of a preoccupation with self. The author of *The Cloud of Unknowing* takes sharp exception to this notion, asserting instead that contemplation is the most perfect expression of concern for others:

> Your fellow men are marvelously enriched by this work of yours, even if you may not fully understand how; the souls in purgatory are touched, for their suffering is eased by the effects of this work; and, of course, your own spirit is purified and strengthened by this contemplative work more than by all others put together.[11]

Certainly this is the experience of those who actually practice contemplation. Within the depths of the contemplative's being, all being is realized. Mutual life is experienced so intensely that an "other" ceases to exist. The suffering of any person is the suffering of the contemplative; the joy of others is the contemplative's joy. Love for others ceases to be a commandment, becoming instead, a natural consequent of an experience of the one Divine Life.

> In the contemplative work itself, he does not distinguish between friend and enemy, brother and stranger. I do not mean, however, that he will cease to feel a spontaneous affection toward a few others who are especially close

to him....The point I am making is that during the work of contemplation everyone is equally dear to him since it is God alone who stirs him to love. He loves all men plainly and nakedly for God; and he loves them all as he loves himself.[12]

The one thing that still remains between the contemplative and God is what the author of *The Cloud of Unknowing* calls the "perception of being." In the course of the practice of contemplation, you will find that there is something at the base of all your thoughts, feelings, and intentions that is itself independent from these things. Thoughts and feelings originate from this ground, but they are not the ground itself. The author of *The Cloud of Unknowing* calls this base an awareness of "being."

While practicing with a word, you may come to an experience of "I am." This is not an awareness of who or where you are, but simply of being. In this awareness, there is the experience of being and the experience of self. In contemplation, however, the "one who experiences" this "I" must be left behind so that the Divine Life itself can shine through. This is not accomplished by an act of will, but by practicing as before. Regarding this point in the practice, the author of *The Cloud of Unknowing* says:

And so reject the thought and experience of all created things but most especially learn to forget yourself, for all your knowledge and experience depends upon the knowledge and feeling of yourself. All else is easily forgotten in comparison with one's own self. See if experience does not prove me right. Long after you have successfully forgotten every creature and its works, you will find that a naked knowing and feeling of your own being still remains between you and your God. And believe me, you will not be perfect in love until this, too, is destroyed.[13]

And so, go down to the deepest point of your mind and think of yourself in this simple, elemental way. (Others will mean the same thing, but because of their experience, speak of the mind's "pinnacle," and of this awareness as the "highest" human wisdom.) In any case, do not think *what you are* but *that you are*. For I grant that to realize what you are demands the effort of your intelligence in a good deal of thought and subtle introspection. But this you have done for quite a while with the help of God's grace; and you understand to some degree just what you really are—a human being by nature and a pitiful, fallen wretch through sin. Well do you know this. Yes, and probably you feel that you know only too well, from experience, the defilements that follow and befall a man because of sin. Fie on them! Forget them, I pray you. Reflect on them no further for fear of contamination. Instead, remember that you also possess an innate ability to know *that you are*, and that you can experience this without any special natural or acquired genius.[14]

But now I want you to understand that although in the beginning I told you to forget everything save the blind awareness of your naked being, I intended all along to lead you eventually to the point where you would forget even this, so as to experience only the being of God. It was with an eye to this ultimate experience that I said in the beginning: *God is your being*....With perseverance in this practice, I expected you to grow increasingly refined in singleness of heart until you were ready to strip, spoil, and utterly unclothe your self-awareness of everything, even the elemental awareness of your own being, so that you might be newly clothed in the gracious stark experience of God as he is in himself.[15]

And so, when in this work you become aware that you are perceiving and experiencing self and not God, be filled with sincere sorrow and long with all your heart to be entirely absorbed in the experience of God alone. Cease not to desire the loss of that pitiful knowledge and corrupted awareness of your blind being. Long to flee from self as from a poison. Forget and disregard your self as ruthlessly as the Lord demands....For wherever you are, in whatever you do, or howsoever you try, that elemental sense of your own blind being will remain between you and your God. It is possible, of course, that God may intervene at times and fill you with a transient experience of himself. Yet outside these moments this naked awareness of your blind being will continually weigh you down and be as a barrier between you and your God, just as in the beginning of this work the various details of your being were like a barrier to the direct awareness of your self. It is then that you will realize how heavy and painful is the burden of self. May Jesus help you in that hour, for you will have great need of him.[16]

This phase of the practice of contemplation, in which the ego self is experienced as a terrible burden, is addressed by all the writers within the Christian contemplative tradition and by the great Eastern traditions as well. Saint John of the Cross calls it the "dark night." It seems to be an indispensable part of this process and is something we will consider again in later chapters.

Consolations

Throughout this difficult part of the journey, you will receive great "consolations" that encourage you to continue on. These sweet spaces of relief, however, constitute danger: you may attempt to cling to these consolations and, as a result, abandon the process itself. This would be like stopping an expedition to a mountaintop at some nice view along the way. All contemplative writers warn against giving in to this temptation, encouraging you to be especially faithful to your practice during this time. The author of *The Cloud of Unknowing* cautions:

I hope you see now why it is so important that we concentrate our whole energy and attention on this gentle stirring of love in the will. With all due reverence for God's gifts, it is my opinion that we should be quite careless of all delights and consolations of sense or spirit, regardless of how pleasurable or sublime they may be. If they come, welcome them but do not rest in them for fear of growing weak; believe me, you will expend a good deal of energy if you remain long in sweet feelings and tears. Possibly too, you may begin to love God on their account and not for himself. You will know whether or not this is happening if you become upset and irritable when you do not experience them. Should you find this to be the case, then your love is not yet chaste or perfect. When love is chaste and perfect, it may allow the senses to be nourished and strengthened by sweet emotions and tears, but it is never troubled if God permits them to disappear. It continues to rejoice in God all the same.[17]

If you practice only for the half hour each day that you sit on your cushion or chair, you will miss the point. Likewise, if your prayer remains only a mental activity, it will cease when your mind is engaged in the necessary tasks of everyday life. Once you've practiced for a period of time, your prayer may gain its own momentum and continue day and night, beyond your conscious control. When it has become a permanent part of your personality, part of your very flesh and bones, you will be firmly established on this contemplative path.

As I have already explained to you, this simple work is not a rival to your daily activities. For with your attention centered on the blind awareness of your naked being united to God's, you will go about your daily rounds, eating and drinking, sleeping and waking, going and coming, speaking and listening, lying down and rising up, standing and kneeling, running and riding, working and resting. In the midst of it all, you will be offering to God continually each day the most precious gift you can make. This work will be at the heart of everything you do, whether active or contemplative....*Your sleep will be untroubled*...and bring deep spiritual strength and nourishment to renew both your body and your spirit.[18]

Meister Eckhart

Meister Eckhart, a Dominican mystic and scholar, died in Germany between 1327 and 1329. Again and again, Eckhart returns to the fundamental theme of the "divine birth" that must take place within each person treading the contemplative path. He is adamant that this birth can only occur through the grace of God, not through any individual human efforts or merits. In fact, writes Eckhart, the more one "seeks" God, the further one strays from finding God. One should seek God so as to find him nowhere. In other words, seek God not, and you will find him.

Eckhart says that striving for God leads us away from God, and a desire for the eternal birth hinders it. Are we, then, at the mercy of an arbitrary God? What is the relationship between divine grace and personal effort?

There is a great paradox here; on the contemplative path we must channel all our energy into this process, and at the same time give up all personal desire and ambition. It is only to the extent that we can walk this way, free of every egocentric concern, that we will be prepared for the divine birth to occur. In fact, this letting go of self *is* the effort we must exert. For our preparedness and the infusion of grace is, finally, one action. Writes Eckhart, "It is one instant, the being ready and the pouring in. When nature reaches her highest point...God enters without hesitation or delay."[19] Therefore, must God give himself to a solitary heart.

When Eckhart writes of the solitary heart, or of poverty or detachment, he refers to much the same state as does the old Christian term *puritas cordis*: purity of heart. This state of mind is essential for one who takes the contemplative path. "Purity," here, does not refer to any moral state, but rather to the letting go of egocentric desires, images, and concepts. In his Conference One, Cassian writes, "The aim of our profession is the...kingdom of heaven. But our point of reference, our objective, is a clean heart, without which it is impossible for anyone to reach the target."[20]

Eckhart speaks often of the "mode-less-ness" of the contemplative path. Only the eye that is absolutely colorless itself, he writes, may see all colors clearly.[21] God and things as they are, are comprehensible only when nothing stands in their way. Only when we are completely empty may we be occasions of the divine birth.

Some have interpreted Eckhart's comments about this "mode-less-ness" to imply that there is no way at all into contemplative experience. Actually, Eckhart says that it is essential that one attain this purity of heart by "passing on a little further" beyond all things:

> The Bride says in the Book of Love: "When I had passed on a little further, I found Him that my soul loves." The *little* that she passed by was all creatures. Whoever does not put them behind him will not find God. She also means that however subtle, however pure a thing is that I know God by, yet it must go. Even the light that is truly God, if I take it where it touches my soul, that is still not right. I must take it there, where it wells forth. I could not properly see the light that shines on the wall unless I turned my gaze to where it comes from. And even then, if I take it where it wells forth, I must be free of this welling forth: I must take it where it rests in itself. And yet I say even that is wrong. I must take it neither where it touches nor where it wells forth nor where it rests in itself, for these are still all modes. We must take God as mode without mode, and essence without essence, for he has no modes. Therefore St. Bernard says, "He who would know thee, God, must measure thee without measure."[22]

Elsewhere Eckhart speaks of this condition as "poverty." He distinguishes between voluntary poverty—which he calls good and endorses as an imitation of Christ's life on earth—and that poverty spoken of in the first beatitude: "Blessed are the poor in spirit, for theirs is the kingdom of heaven" (Matthew 5:3). Eckhart is primarily interested in the second kind of poverty, as he writes at length in Sermon 87:

> Firstly, we say that a poor man is one who *wants* nothing. There are some who do not properly understand the meaning of this: these are the people who cling with attachment to penances and outward practices, making much of these. May God have mercy on such folk for understanding so little of divine truth! These people are called holy from their outward appearances, but inwardly they are asses, for they are ignorant of the actual nature of divine truth. These people say that a poor man is one who wants nothing and they explain it this way: A man should so live that he never does his own will in anything, but should strive to do the dearest will of God. It is well with these people because their intention is right, and we commend them for it....
>
> If, then, I were asked what *is* a poor man who wants nothing, I should reply as follows. As long as a man is so disposed that it is his *will* with which he would do the most beloved will of God, that man has not the poverty we are speaking about: for that man has a *will* to serve God's will—and that is not true poverty! For a man to possess true poverty, he must be as free of his created will as he was when he was not. For I declare by the eternal truth, as long as you have the *will* to do the will of God, and longing for eternity and God, you are not poor: for a poor man is one who wills nothing and desires nothing....

Secondly, he is a poor man who *knows* nothing. We have sometimes said that a man should live as if he did not live either for himself, or for truth, or for God. But now we will speak differently and go further, and say: For a man to possess *this* poverty he must live so that he is *unaware* that he does not live for himself, or for truth, or for God. He must be so lacking in all knowledge that he neither knows nor recognizes nor feels that God lives in him: more still, he must be free of all the understanding that lives in him. For when that man stood in the eternal being of God, nothing *else* lived in him: what lived there was himself. Therefore we declare that a man should be as free from his own knowledge as he was when he was not. That man should let God work as He will, and himself stand idle....

I have said before, the poor man is not he who wants to fulfil the will of God but he who lives in such a way as to be free of his own will and of God's will, as he was when he was not. Of this poverty we declare that it is the *highest* poverty. Secondly, we have said he is a poor man who does not know of the working of God within him. He who stands as free of knowledge and understanding as God stands of all things, has the *purest* poverty. But the third is the *straitest* poverty of which we shall now speak: that is when a man *has* nothing.

Now pay earnest attention to this! I have often said, and eminent authorities say it too, that a man should be so free of all things and all works, both inward and outward, that he may be a proper abode for God where God can work. Now we shall say something else. If it is the case that a man is free of all creatures, of God and of self, and if it is still the case that God finds a place *in him* to work, then we declare that as long as this is *in* that man, he is not poor with the strictest poverty. For it is not God's intention in His works that a man should have a place within himself for God to work in: for poverty of spirit means being so free of God and all His works, that God, if He wishes to work in the soul, is Himself the place where He works—and this He gladly does. For, if he finds a man *so* poor, then God performs His own work, and the man is passive to God within him, and God is His own place of work, being a worker in Himself. It is just here, in *this* poverty, that man enters into that eternal essence that once he was, that he is now and evermore shall remain....

So we say that a man should be so poor that he neither is nor has any place [in which] God [may] work. To preserve a place is to preserve distinction. Therefore I pray to God to make me free of God, for my essential being is above God, taking God as the origin of creatures. For in that essence of God in which God is above being and distinction, there I was myself and knew myself so as to make this man....

The masters say God is a being, an intellectual being that knows all things. But we say God is not a being and not intellectual and does not know this or that. Thus God is free of all things, and so He *is* all things. To be poor in spirit, a man must be poor of all his own knowledge: not knowing any *thing*, not God, nor creature nor himself....

A great master says that his breaking-through is nobler than his emanation, and this is true. When I flowed forth from God, all creatures declared: "There is a God;" but *this* cannot make me blessed, for with this I acknowledge myself as a creature. But in my breaking-through, where I stand free of my own will, of God's will, of all His works, and of God himself, *then* I am above all creatures and am neither God nor creature, but I am that which I was and shall remain for evermore. There I shall receive an imprint that will raise me above all the angels. By this imprint I shall gain such wealth that I shall not be content with God inasmuch as He is God, or with all His divine works: for this breaking-through guarantees to me that I and God are one. *Then* I am what I was, then I neither wax nor wane, for then I am an unmoved cause that moves all things. Here, God finds no place *in* man, for man by his poverty wins for himself what he has eternally been and shall eternally remain. Here, God is one with the spirit, and that is the strictest poverty one can find.

If anyone cannot understand this sermon, he need not worry. For so long as a man is not equal to this truth, he *cannot* understand my words, for this is a naked truth which has come direct from the heart of God.

That we may so live as to experience it eternally, may God help us. Amen.[23]

In "Talks of Instruction," Eckhart speaks further of the inner state, the "purity of heart" that is the path of perfection. Here he uses the term *solitude*. He is careful to explain, however, that this particular kind of solitude has nothing at all to do with running away from other people or from the activities of everyday life:

Those who do well, do well wherever they are, and in

whatever company, and those who do badly, do badly wherever they are and in whatever company. But if a man does well, God is really in him, and with him everywhere, on the streets and among people, just as much as in church, or a desert place, or a cell. If he really has God, and only God, then nothing disturbs him....since God cannot be distracted by the numbers of things, neither can the person, for he is one in One, in which all divided things are gathered up to unity and there undifferentiated.

One ought to keep hold of God in everything and accustom his mind to retain God always among his feelings, thoughts, and loves. Take care how you think of God. As you think of him in church or closet, think of him everywhere. Take him with you among the crowds and turmoil of the alien world. As I have said so often, speaking of uniformity, we do not mean that one should regard all deeds, places, and people as interchangeable. That would be a great mistake; for it is better to pray than to spin and the church ranks above the street. You should, however, maintain the same mind, the same trust, the same earnestness toward God in all your doings. Believe me, if you keep this kind of evenness, nothing can separate you from God-consciousness.

On the other hand, the person who is not conscious of God's presence, but who must always be going out to get him from this and that, who has to seek him by special methods, as by means of some activity, person, or place—such people have not attained God. It can easily happen that they are disturbed, for they have not God and they do not seek, think, and love only him, and therefore, not only will evil company be to them a stumbling block, but good company as well—not only the street, but the church; not only bad deeds and words, but good ones as well. The difficulty lies within the man for whom God has not yet become everything. If God were everything, the man would get along well wherever he went and among whatever people, for he would possess God and no one could rob him or disturb his work....

It is like learning to write. To acquire this art, one must practice much, however disagreeable or difficult it may be, however impossible it may seem. Practicing earnestly and often, one learns to write, acquires the art. To be sure, each letter must first be considered separately and accurately, reproduced over and over again; but once having acquired skill, one need not pay any attention to the reproduction [of the letters] or even think of them. He will write fluently and freely whether it be penmanship or some bold work, in which his art appears. It is sufficient for the writer to know that he is using his skill and since he does not always have to think of it, he does his work by means of it.

So a man should shine with the divine Presence without having to work at it.[24]

Eckhart preaches that God experiences himself as God in every activity. God is God within us—our feelings, thoughts, and perceptions. God is God in others and in the thousand things of nature. Contemplative experience is simply the experience of this divine dynamic from within. "If you can understand it," writes Eckhart, "you will be able to grasp my meaning and get to the bottom of all that I have ever preached about."[25] For this is indeed the crux of mystical experience: that an indescribable unity exists between God and humanity and all that is. In Sermon 60, Eckhart points toward this unity, using the analogy of the human eye seeing a piece of wood:

> When my eye is open it is an eye: when it is shut it is still the same eye; and the wood is neither more nor less by reason of my seeing it. Now mark me well: Suppose my eye, being one and single in itself, falls on the wood with vision, then though each thing stays as it is, yet in the very act of seeing they are so much at one that we can really say "eye-wood," and the wood *is* my eye. Now, if the wood were free from matter and wholly immaterial as my eyesight is, then we could truly say that in the act of seeing the wood and my eye were of one essence. If this is true of material things, it is all the more true of spiritual.[26]

Elsewhere Eckhart writes, "The eye with which I see God is the same eye with which God sees me."[27]

There are many analogies that point toward this identity of the relative and the Absolute. Consider the hurricane, for example. At its center, the hurricane is absolutely tranquil; and yet it is here, at the eye of the storm, that its great force originates. These two aspects of the hurricane are, of course, inseparable. Without the eye, there could be no storm; and with only the eye, no storm would exist. And so it is with Divine Life. We must experience it both in its tranquillity and in its dynamic. Or, more precisely, we must experience its tranquillity *within* its dynamic. As Zen says, form *is* emptiness, emptiness *is* form. So, too, divine life cannot be experienced only in its essence, but must always be experienced in some expression—in form.

And how is it that one comes into this experience? Always, says Eckhart, through detachment and poverty. Much afraid, he ponders the utter detachment the soul must experience to attain union with God.

As long as any distinction of any created things can look into the soul, she is disconsolate. I say, as I have often said before, so far as the soul's created nature goes, there is no such thing as truth. I say there is something higher than the soul's created nature. But some priests cannot understand how there can be anything so nearly akin to God, and so *one*. It has [nothing] in common with anything. All that is created or creaturely is alien. It is a single one in itself, and takes in nothing from outside.[28]

It is only when we attain this solitude and detachment, says Eckhart, that we take our proper place in the world. Here the divine dynamic is, as it were, experienced from within. Here, in Saint Paul's words, "It is no longer I who live, but it is Christ who lives in me" (Galatians 2:20).

Where creatures stop, God begins to be. Now all God wants of you is for you to go out of yourself in the way of creatureliness and let God be within you. The least creaturely image that takes shape in you is as big as God. How is that? [Because this image] deprives you of the whole of God. As soon as [it] comes in, God has to leave with all His godhead. But when the image goes out, God comes in. God desires you to go out of yourself (as creature) as much as if all his blessedness depended on it. My dear friend, what harm can it do you to do God the favor of letting Him be God in you?[29]

John of the Cross

In sixteenth-century Spain, Saint John of the Cross taught and wrote on the transformative experiences encountered in contemplative practice. In his introduction to *The Ascent of Mount Carmel,* John writes, "This treatise explains how to reach divine union quickly."[30] Indeed, this is the whole thrust of his teaching.

> The individual...should proceed only with a loving attention to God, without making specific acts. He should conduct himself passively...without efforts of his own, but with the simple, loving awareness, as a person who opens his eyes with loving attention.[31]

This "loving attention," referred to elsewhere in his writings as "loving knowledge" or "passive loving receptivity," is the heart of John's way. It describes an inward listening that must displace all other activities of the mind.

> A person...should be very free and annihilated regarding all things, because any thought or discursive reflection or satisfaction upon which he may want to lean would impede and disquiet him, and make noise in the profound silence of his senses and his spirit, which he possesses for the sake of this deep and delicate listening. God speaks to the heart in this solitude.[32]

God's light is always within us, writes John. But because our intellect, sense, and will are so overbearing, we are unable to experience this light. "It is so delicate that a person...is unable to feel this incomprehensible new experience." Accordingly, writes John, it is only through a complete disengagement of memory, intellect, and will that we are able to at last perceive the divine life that is within us from the beginning.

A person can with the greatest ease disturb and hinder these anointings by no more than the least act he may desire of his memory, intellect or will, or by making use of his senses, appetite, knowledge, or his own satisfaction and pleasure. This is all seriously harmful.[33]

In Jesus' farewell discourse in the Gospel of John, he says to his disciples, "Nevertheless I tell you the truth: it is to your advantage that I go away, for if I do not go away, the Advocate will not come to you" (John 16:7). John of the Cross interprets this passage to mean that the historical Jesus must depart so that the Christ within each of us may emerge. He considers the risen Christ's words to Mary Magdalene, "Do not hold on to me" (John 20:17), to be addressed to all of us and to mean:

One should not desire to clutch sensory communications nor suffer encumbrance from them, since they are what most derogates from faith. Manifestly, these visions and sense apprehensions cannot serve as a means for union since they bear no proportion to God. This was one of the reasons for Christ's not wanting Mary Magdalen or St. Thomas to touch Him.

The devil is most pleased when he sees that a man desires to admit revelations. For then he has an excellent opportunity to inject errors and disparage faith. As I have declared, a man desiring these apprehensions becomes coarse in his faith and even exposes himself to many temptations.[34]

Such statements clearly encourage us to set forth on the contemplative path even when we no longer derive satisfaction from imaginative prayer and sensory meditation. At the beginning of our contemplative practice, a great deal of discipline is required to avoid lapsing into mental activity or drowsiness. It is only through the continual practice of loving awareness that the path, at last, becomes a permanent part of our personalities.

Many acts, in no matter what area, will engender a habit. Similarly, the repetition of many particular acts of this loving knowledge becomes so continuous that a habit is formed in the soul.[35]

Regular practice is the foundation of the contemplative path. We know that John often prayed for nights on end. He liked to pray outdoors or before open windows. In yoga and Zen, students sit for no less than ten hours a day during their regular retreats.

Prayer, however, cannot end when we rise from our cushions or chairs and go on with our daily lives. It is not until "a habit is formed in the soul" that we have firmly established ourselves on the contemplative path. This may sound like a great deal of "work" on our parts, and certainly specific acts of will are part of this path. But in a more fundamental sense, there is nothing that we can "do" at all to enter into transmental experience. We can only become empty, only let go of all that obscures the knowledge of who we really are.

John of the Cross speaks often to this emptying, or letting go. He writes that a soul who is full of things is devoid of God, while a soul who is devoid of things is filled with God. In *The Ascent of Mount Carmel*, John compares Christ's total emptying of himself on the cross to the work that must occur within each of us before we experience divine life. We, too, must be detached from all material and spiritual things, including all consolations and ecstatic experience. Zen teachers speak of the necessity of "dying on one's cushion," and John of the Cross would certainly concur.

In a diagram depicting the ascent of Mount Carmel, John labels the steps upward as *nada, nada, nada*: "nothing, nothing, nothing." At the top of the mountain, John writes *Y en el monte, nada*: "And even on the mountain—nothing." In fact, on such an ascent, we may be so stricken and forsaken by God that we indeed feel a kind of death is taking place. This is the contemplative path, a path that is oftentimes very painful, requiring, as it does, the complete transcendence of our ego selves. John has written vividly of the kind of suffering this process can entail, and we will look closely at what he has to say in a later chapter.

But for all that John says about killing and death, the path he outlines is fundamentally a way of liberation and life. There is certainly a great deal that must pass away in this process, but these "deaths" never take place for their own sakes, only that the divine life may shine forth. At the outset, we may be so wrapped up in our own desires, ideas, and past experiences that we are possessed by them. Our inability to clear away these hindrances can intensify into tremendous suffering. They constitute, as it were, a wall of glass behind which our beloved lies—within grasp, but unreachable. At this point, writes John, there is nothing more we can "do" to achieve the union we desire. Rather, we must remain completely passive, continuing with our loving attention, while God takes over and purifies us from within. In Chapter 7 of *The Ascent of Mount Carmel*, John writes:

This chalice symbolizes death to one's natural self through denudation and annihilation. As a result of this death, a man is able to walk along the narrow path in the sensitive part of his soul....On this road there is room only for self-denial (as our Savior asserts) and the cross. The cross is a supporting staff and greatly lightens and eases the journey.

Our Lord proclaimed through Saint Matthew: *My yoke is sweet and my burden (the cross) light* [Matthew 11:30]. If a man resolutely submits to the carrying of this cross, if he decidedly wants to find and endure trial in all things for God, he will discover in all of them great relief and sweetness. This will be so because he journeys the road denuded of all and with no desire for anything. If he aims after the possession of something, from God or elsewhere, his journey will not be one of nakedness and detachment.[36]

According to John of the Cross, each of us is confronted with precisely the challenge that Christ himself faced: that of becoming a true image of God. We are all required to let divine life become manifest in us without obstruction. The process of redemption is, ultimately, the process of "becoming Christ," the process of becoming a whole human being. Accordingly, writes John:

I should not consider any spirituality worthwhile that would walk in sweetness and ease and run from the imitation of Christ. Because I have said that Christ is the way and that this way is a death to our natural selves in the sensory and spiritual parts of the soul, I would like to demonstrate how this death is patterned on Christ's. For He is our model and light.

First, during His life, He died spiritually to the sensitive part, and at His death He died naturally. He proclaimed during His life that He had no place whereon to lay His head [Matthew 8:20]. And at His death He had less.

Second, at the moment of His death He was certainly annihilated in His soul, without any consolation or relief, since the Father left Him that way in innermost aridity in the lower part. He was thereby compelled to cry out: *My God, My God, why have you forsaken me?* [Matthew 27:46]. This was the most extreme abandonment, sensitively, that He had suffered in His life. And by it He accomplished the most marvelous work of His whole life....The Lord achieved this, as I say, at the moment in which He was most annihilated in all things.[37]

While John writes often of the suffering that accompanies this way, he also writes eloquently, particularly in his poetry, of the unspeakable happiness that at last breaks forth with the emergence of the divine life.

For this awakening is a movement of the Word in the substance of the soul, containing such grandeur, dominion, glory, and intimate sweetness that it seems to the soul that all the balsams and fragrant spices and flowers of the world are commingled, stirred, and shaken so as to yield their sweet odor, and that all the kingdoms and dominions of the world and all the powers and virtues of heaven are moved; and not only this, but it also seems that all the virtues and substances and perfections and graces of every created thing glow and make the same movement all at once.[38]

Taken as a whole, John's writings reveal a man not at all at odds with or scornful of creation. For all his emphasis on detachment, John clearly took great delight in the material world, particularly in nature. In *The Living Flame of Love,* John gives us the reason for this delight: in all things, he experienced only God:

And here lies the remarkable delight of this awakening: the soul knows creatures through God and not God through creatures. This amounts to knowing the effects through their cause and not the cause through its effects.[39]

A final theme—one to which John returns time and again—is the incompetence of many spiritual directors when it comes to leading people along the contemplative way. It has been suggested that the principal reason John wrote as much as he did was the lack of competent guidance available to people in their spiritual lives. It seems that many spiritual directors in John's time had no personal contemplative experience, and that those who did were fearful of counseling others because of the Inquisition.

As a result, John frequently takes his contemporaries to task, calling them "blind men who lead blind men...little foxes that destroy flourishing vineyards...the builders of the tower of Babel...crude forgers who are only able to hammer...(and) people who construct obstacles at the gate of heaven."[40] In *The Living Flame of Love,* John writes:

God becomes extremely indignant with such directors and...promises them chastisement: *You ate the milk of my flock and you covered yourself with their wool and did not feed my flock; I will,* He says, *seek my flock at your hand* [Ezekiel 34:3,10].[41]

John's principal complaint regarding his fellow directors is that when students approached the point of finally stepping forward into emptiness, the directors led them back into discursive meditation and other devotional practices. When inner dryness and loneliness set in, writes John, it is the role of the director to encourage people to continue out into the desert where, at length, they may finally come to know their God. But in John's time—and today, too—many directors had little or no experience of this contemplative path themselves and so tended to thwart the progress of others.

John considered competent guidance an indispensable part of the contemplative journey. He was often indignant with the weak spiritual lives and simple ignorance of other directors.

Perhaps in their zeal these directors err with good will because they do not know any better. Not for this reason, however, should they be excused for the counsels they give rashly, without first understanding the road and spirit a person may be following, and for rudely meddling in something they do not understand, instead of leaving the matter to one who does understand.[42]

It is very important that a person, desiring to advance in recollection and perfection, take care into whose hands he entrusts himself, for the disciple will become like the master, and as is the father so will be the son.[43]

Only the one who has already taken this path will be able to provide responsible guidance for others. One of the principal characteristics of such a guide, writes John, is an appreciation of the limits of this role.

> These directors should reflect that they themselves are not the chief agent, guide, and mover of souls in this matter, but that the principal guide is the Holy Spirit, Who is never neglectful of souls, and that they are instruments for directing them to perfection through faith and the law of God, according to the spirit God gives each one.
>
> Thus the director's whole concern should not be to accommodate souls to his own method and condition, but he should observe the road along which God is leading them, and if he does not recognize it, he should leave them alone and not bother them.[44]

John speaks, too, of the unrealistic expectations that a student may have of a spiritual guide. It is a problem that arises today, especially among the so-called "New Age religions." In many of these, the teacher is considered one's savior. The contemplative path, however, has no place for "saviors" and gurus; any responsible guide will refuse deification and help the student understand that spiritual direction is solely a matter of removing those obstacles that prevent God from taking effect in the soul. The guide, writes John, is like John the Baptist, who was not himself the Bridegroom but only one who pointed the way.

For John, a spiritual guide is not someone who applies a fixed formula in every case. Rather, he insists that each person receive individual guidance according to his or her unique abilities and needs. At the canonization proceedings for John of the Cross, one of his students (Joseph of Jesus) testified to the importance of this point in John's spiritual direction:

He readily gained insight into two things without which no spiritual master can safely lead those whom he is directing: to know the tastes and the maturity of each of the souls, and to recognize what God wanted of them in order to lead them in a reasonable and secure manner.[45]

An essential part of this gift of "discernment," writes John, is a director's ability to apply rational thought and sound, natural judgment. These qualities hold in check a student's inclinations to blindly follow his or her own experience.

God is so content that the rule and direction of man be through other men, and that a person be governed by natural reason, that He definitely does not want us to bestow entire credence upon His supernatural communications, or be confirmed in their strength and security until they pass through this human channel of the mouth of man. As often as He reveals something to a person, He confers upon his soul a kind of inclination to manifest this to the appropriate person. Until a man does this, he usually goes without complete satisfaction, for he has not received it from another man like himself.[46]

Finally, John of the Cross cautions all directors against holding people back from the "dark night."

Once a person has begun to enter this simple and idle state of contemplation, which comes about when he can no longer meditate, he should not at any time or season engage in meditations or look for support in spiritual savor or satisfaction, but stand upright on his own feet, with his spirit completely detached from everything.[47]

Do not say, therefore: "Oh, the soul does not advance, because it is not doing anything." For if it is true that it is not doing anything, I shall prove to you that it is accomplishing a great deal by doing nothing. If the intellect empties itself of particular knowledge, natural or spiritual, it advances, and the freer it becomes of particular knowledge and acts of understanding, the further it advances in its journey toward the supreme, supernatural Good.[48]

In this delicate state along the contemplative path, John urges spiritual directors to limit their guidance to bringing each student to

as complete a withdrawal and solitude as possible, for the more solitude he obtains and the nearer he approaches this idle tranquillity, the more abundantly will the spirit of divine wisdom be infused into his soul. This wisdom is loving, tranquil, solitary, peaceful, mild, and an inebriator of the spirit, by which the soul feels tenderly and gently wounded and carried away, without knowing by whom, nor from where, nor how.[49]

When a student has attained such a state, writes John, the director—and indeed, the student as well—has done all that is humanly possible to prepare for the Bridegroom's coming.

Chapter 3

The
Purification
Process

The contemplative path is never without its difficulties. The first is usually the discovery that we are not the master of our own house, that it is the ego that masters—tyrannizes—us much of the time. The ego constantly furnishes us with thoughts, feelings, and desires, making it nearly impossible to hold only our word in awareness. Even when we learn to persist with the practice, we will not necessarily become calm. Fear, aggression, and other disturbing contents of the unconscious often arise and become obstacles to our continued practice.

All of the great contemplative writers speak of the difficulties we encounter along this way. The first time a man looks inward, cautions the author of *The Cloud of Unknowing*, the sins of his whole life rise up before him. No evil thought, word, or deed remains hidden. Mysteriously and darkly they are burned into (him)…

At times the sight is as terrible as a glimpse of hell and he is tempted to despair of ever being healed and relieved of his sore burden. Many arrive at this juncture in the interior life but the terrible, comfortless agony they experience facing themselves drives them back to thoughts of worldly pleasures. They seek without for relief in things of the flesh, unable to bear the spiritual emptiness within. But they have not understood that they were not ready for the spiritual comfort which would have succored them had they waited.[1]

John of the Cross has written in great detail of the "dark night," a time of dryness and darkening of the intellect and senses along the contemplative path. Intellect, memory, and will play no active part in this purification process; emotions, too, must be allowed to pass by. Because they lack the ability to function on the higher level of consciousness which is about to open up, these faculties must be abandoned, or more accurately, they are "darkened" and not helpful for experiencing God. In Book Two, Chapter 3 of *The Dark Night*, John of the Cross explains:

God divests the faculties, affections, and senses, both spiritual and sensory, interior and exterior. He leaves the intellect in darkness, the will in aridity, the memory in emptiness, and the affections in supreme affliction, bitterness, and anguish, by depriving the soul of the feeling and satisfaction it previously obtained from spiritual blessings. For this privation is one of the conditions required that the spiritual form, which is the union of love, may be introduced in the spirit and united with it. The Lord works all of this in the soul by means of a pure and dark contemplation...this night is the principal purification of the soul.[2]

A transition is being made to a new level of consciousness in which knowing is not mediated by the senses or intellect, but by a direct intuitive vision. It is loving awareness that knows nothing and wants nothing. John of the Cross describes it as a transformation process. The dark night, writes John, has much the same effect on the soul as

> fire has on...wood. The soul is purged and prepared for union with the divine light just as the wood is prepared for transformation into the fire. Fire, when applied to wood, first dehumidifies it, dispelling all moisture and making it give off any water it contains. Then it gradually turns the wood black, makes it dark and ugly, and even causes it to emit a bad odor. By drying out the wood, the fire brings to light and expels all those ugly and dark accidents which are contrary to fire. Finally, by heating and enkindling it from without, the fire transforms the wood into itself and makes it as beautiful as it is itself. Once transformed, the wood no longer has any activity or passivity of its own, except for its weight and its quantity which is denser than the fire. For it possesses the properties and performs the actions of fire: it is dry and it dries; it is hot and it gives off heat; it is brilliant and it illumines; and it is also light, much lighter than before....
>
> Similarly, we should philosophize about this divine, loving fire of contemplation. Before transforming the

soul, it purges it of all contrary qualities. It produces blackness and darkness and brings to the fore the soul's ugliness; thus the soul seems worse than before and unsightly and abominable. This divine purge stirs up all the foul and vicious humors of which the soul was never before aware; never did it realize there was so much evil in itself, since these humors were so deeply rooted. And now that they may be expelled and annihilated they are brought to light and seen clearly through the illumination of this dark light of divine contemplation. Although the soul is no worse than before, neither in itself nor in its relationship with God, it feels undoubtedly so bad as to be not only unworthy that God should see it but deserving of His abhorrence; in fact, it feels that God now does abhor it.[3]

The purification process can be terribly painful, a time of helplessness, pain, desperation, panic, and horror. Only one who has gone through it can know what it means. This suffering, writes John, occurs not for its own sake, but in order to prepare the soul for the union that it seeks. Hence the dark night

strikes in order to renew the soul and divinize it (by stripping it of the habitual affections and properties of the old man to which it is strongly united, attached and conformed), it so disentangles and dissolves the spiritual substance—absorbing it in a profound darkness—that the soul at the sight of its miseries feels that it is melting away and being undone by a cruel spiritual death; it feels as if it were swallowed by a beast and being digested in the dark belly, and it suffers an anguish comparable to

Jonas's when in the belly of the whale [Jonah 2:1-3]. It is fitting that the soul be in this sepulcher of dark death in order that it attain the spiritual resurrection for which it hopes.[4]

In Book Two, Chapter 6 of *The Dark Night,* John gives an inkling of the suffering one may encounter in the course of this process and the reason the mystics call this period *horror vacui:* the horror of emptiness. The soul, he writes, feels itself in "the shadow of death," amidst "the sighs of death, and the sorrows of hell, all of which reflect the feeling of God's absence." The soul "also feels forsaken and despised by creatures, particularly by his friends," a "spiritual emptiness an oppressive undoing and an inner torment." John warns that "sometimes this experience is so vivid that it seems to the soul that it sees hell and perdition open before it."[5]

The contemplative path is, in part, a path of suffering because it demands purification and surrender. All attachments to the limited sense of self must be relinquished so that the divine life can shine forth unobstructed in us. Resistance to this emptying produces suffering in the form of physical and psychic pain.

As a result of this pain, and the temptation to abandon the path because of it, we need constant help and encouragement. We need someone to help us understand and accept the suffering as an important part of this spiritual path. The experience is much like going into the hospital for an operation. Although the patient expects to suffer, recovery is the goal.

The suffering of the dark night is not a meaningless pain, however; it is the process of spiritual purification. Only with this appreciation are we likely to summon the strength necessary to see the process through to its end. Our attitude toward suffering determines its effect on us. Consider, for instance, the case of two people stranded in the desert with nothing but water for four weeks. One experiences deprivation, searches for food, imagines and dreams of food, and becomes weak. The other prepares for a long fast, a time of physical and psychological purification. Approaching the time as a period of fasting allows this person to move through the deprivation strengthened, cleansed, and with a heightened spiritual awareness. The first person, on the other hand, becomes bogged down in despair, fear, and hopelessness. John says to think of this process not as an affliction, but as a grace.

Oh, then, spiritual soul, when you see your appetites darkened, your inclinations dry and constrained, your faculties incapacitated for any interior exercise, do not be afflicted; think of this as a grace, since God is freeing you from yourself and taking from you your own activity. However well your actions may have succeeded you did not work so completely, perfectly, and securely—owing to their impurity and awkwardness—as you do now that God takes you by the hand and guides you in darkness, as though you were blind, along a way and to a place you know not. You would never have succeeded in reaching this place no matter how good your eyes and your feet.

To reach a new and unknown land and travel unknown roads, a man cannot be guided by his own knowledge, rather he has doubts about his own knowledge and seeks the guidance of others. Obviously he cannot reach new territory nor attain this added knowledge if he does not take these new and unknown roads and abandon those familiar ones. Similarly, when a person is learning new details about his art or trade, he must work in darkness and not with what he already knows. If he refuses to lay aside his former knowledge, he will never make any further progress. The soul, too, when it advances, walks in darkness and unknowing.

Since God, as we said, is the master and guide of the soul, this blind man, it can truly rejoice, now that it has come to understand as it has here, and say: in darkness, and secure.[6]

The Shadow

Mystics have always suffered psychologically, and often physically, on the contemplative journey. Because they were able to see meaning in this suffering, not as an end in itself but as a necessary purification, they accepted it humbly and came through their dark night stronger than before.

This is often a long period of grappling with what Jung called the "shadow." *Shadow* is a term for everything that the ego, consciously or unconsciously, has found incompatible with it and has subsequently repressed. The shadow veils what one does not want to see or have others see. Shadow material is not necessarily negative, however. It can contain much that is positive, but it is generally in an underdeveloped form.

Encountering the shadow may be an important work in contemplation for it is a dimension of encountering oneself. Because the shadow material consists of elements that are not reconciled with the conscious self-image, it may interfere with contemplative prayer. When the shadow is integrated into the conscious ego attitude, however, both are transformed and a mature synthesis emerges.

When left unexamined, this shadow material can be overwhelming. It is best if, when we become aware of some thought, feeling, or image, we do not follow it, but simply return to our practice. Some of this material, however, may be significant. It has come into our consciousness for a reason, a reason best pursued outside the time set aside for contemplative practice. It would, of course, be foolish and impossible to look for the genesis of every random thought. We can benefit from using one of the many tools that are especially designed to help us work with particularly strong or persistent thoughts and feelings. Therapy, too, can be helpful, sometimes necessary.

The contemplative path is a healing process, a process that may involve the integration of these neglected aspects. While there are ways that we can actively engage this process, the greatest transformative work must be done *to* us rather than *by* us. Hence, John of the Cross labels this a "passive purification" of the soul, accomplished by God alone. Meister Eckhart notes that the whole scattered world of lower things is gathered up into oneness only when we enter upon a life in which there are no opposites. He prays that we mount from a life divided to a life unified.

Loneliness and Transference

As human beings develop from preconsciousness to ego-consciousness, we become aware of our limitations, helplessness, isolation, and loneliness. Since we cannot bear this condition without what we understand as love, we become fearful and seek safety and security, initially, outside ourselves.

While fear may take many forms, it arises, ultimately, from the experience of separation and isolation, the sense of being cut off from the ground of being, unable to find meaning in life. After eating from the tree of knowledge, man was able to distinguish between good and evil. At that instant, he realized his nakedness; separate and alone, he knew the ache of loneliness and longed to overcome it, to transform his isolation into safety and unity.

This isolation expresses itself in the wish for love and affection. During childhood, we project this longing onto our parents. Later, we may seek fulfillment with a sexual partner. Eventually, however, we realize that a partner will not satisfy that deep ache, that savage longing.

With time, many ideas present themselves in disguise as possible solutions to the problem of loneliness: drugs, alcohol, entertainment, wealth, career, self-sacrificing service. This illusion of safety ends, however, when the effect of the remedy wears off. The desperate loneliness remains and is perhaps even worse.

Finally, when we learn that we cannot find fulfillment in temporal reality, we begin to seek and expect fulfillment from God. "God is the father and I am God's child. I can love God and ask his forgiveness. I must fear him. I feel safe in God's arms. He comforts me when I cry, loves me when I'm well behaved, punishes me when I'm naughty." Projecting the fulfillment of our longing onto a God outside ourselves, we embrace this kind of piety, characteristic of most religions. Such projections are natural aspects of our humanity. It's important, however, that we see through this projection and discover its meaning.

The mystical tradition of all religions is aware of this course of events and counsels us to abandon all images and notions of God. "We ought not to...be satisfied with the God we have thought of, for when the thought slips the mind, that God slips with it. What we want is rather the reality of God, exalted far above any human thought or creature."[7] "Therefore I pray to God to make me free of God."[8]

Psychophysiological Symptoms

In addition to the subconscious material that may arise and produce difficulties along the contemplative path, there is a wide range of psychophysical phenomena that may confront one going this path. Various yogic traditions have made detailed studies of the kinds of energy that can be released when spiritual practice deepens. In fact, an entire branch of yoga, called kundalini yoga, devotes itself to an analysis of these energies and the ways they can be harnessed to further spiritual development. *Kundalini* is a Sanskrit word that means "coiled up." The various yogic traditions propose that this valuable psychic energy is coiled, like a serpent, at the base of the human spine. The goal in many of these disciplines is to awaken this dormant energy and allow it to move upward through the various psychic centers or "chakras" until it unites finally with pure consciousness at the crown of the head.

While the Christian tradition has made no such detailed inquiry into the physical phenomena associated with transmental states of consciousness, Christian literature makes reference to many episodes that parallel the experiences of those going a yogic way. Saint Anthony, one of the first desert mystics, frequently encountered strange and sometimes terrifying psychophysical forces while at prayer. One such vivid episode is recorded by Athanasius in his biography of Saint Anthony.

Girding himself in this way, Anthony went out to the tombs that were situated some distance from the village. He charged one of his friends to supply him periodically with bread, and he entered one of the tombs and remained alone within, his friend having closed the door on him. When the enemy could stand it no longer—for he was apprehensive that Anthony might before long fill the desert with the discipline—approaching one night with a multitude of demons, he whipped him with such force that he lay on the earth, speechless from the tortures. He contended that the pains were so severe as to lead one to say that the blows could not have been delivered by humans, since they caused such agony....But by God's providence, the friend came the next day bringing him the loaves. Opening the door and seeing him lying, as if dead, on the ground, he picked him up and carried him to the Lord's house in the village and laid him on the earth.[9]

Fortunately, psychophysical experiences are seldom so traumatic. Oftentimes they are exceedingly pleasurable; one's whole body may be swept with feelings of well-being and bliss. Whatever form these expressions of psychic power take, they should be considered entirely normal and a positive sign that one is deepening in the practice.

Lee Sannella, the American psychiatrist, has extensively studied the kundalini phenomenon.[10] He breaks down its symptoms into four principal areas: motor, sensory, interpretive, and nonphysiological. The following is a brief summary of Sannella's observations in each of these categories.

Motor: Kundalini often interferes with the normal motor functions of the body. Breathing may become extremely shallow or very deep and prolonged. Part or all of the body may jerk uncontrollably, occasionally with downright gymnastic effect. During prayer, Therese of Lisieux would reportedly spring from her knees onto her head without the use of her hands. At times, a kind of paralysis might occur or the body may spontaneously assume classic yogic postures.

Sensory: During deep meditation, it's not unusual for a person to hear various sounds ranging from music or voices to a high-pitched whistle or roar. One might see inner lights of various hues and intensities. The skin may become quite warm or very cold. Tingling sensations might spread across the skin or throughout the entire body.

Interpretive: In the course of prolonged meditation, previously unknown mental processes may arise. Emotions ranging from bliss to utter terror may take hold. One's thought process might speed up dramatically, become extremely slow, or stop altogether. Sometimes one feels entirely detached from all that is taking place, within oneself and without (a state known to the yogis as "witness consciousness"). Occasionally, one's body may feel like it has become gigantic, many times its normal size.

Nonphysiological: This is Sannella's last and least understood category of kundalini experience. It includes various out-of-body experiences such as astral projection and extraordinary psychic perceptions by means of which a person may be able to describe in great detail an event or location far distant from them at the time.

Sannella draws an important conclusion concerning the benign and beneficial effects of kundalini awakening.

Symptoms, when caused by this process, will disappear spontaneously in time. Because it is essentially a purificatory or balancing process, and each person has only a finite amount of impurities of the sort removed by kundalini, the process is self-limiting. Disturbances seen are therefore not pathological, but rather therapeutic, constituting a removal of potentially pathological elements. The kundalini force arises spontaneously from deep within the mind, and is apparently self-directing. Tension and imbalance thus result, not from the process itself, but from conscious or subconscious interference with it.[11]

While many yogic traditions pay close attention to all aspects of the kundalini process—the purportedly orderly progression of the awakened kundalini energy throughout the human being—writers within the Christian contemplative tradition generally caution against becoming fascinated with such phenomena. They are never considered something to be desired. In fact, some fully mature contemplatives have no experience of them whatsoever. Often, they are more a hindrance than a help to contemplative life. When Anthony awoke on the church floor, he had his friends carry him back to the tomb where he resumed his prayer.

Again he was alone inside. Because of the blows, he was not strong enough to stand, but he prayed while lying down. And after the prayer he yelled out: "Here I am— Anthony! I do not run from your blows, for even if you give me more, nothing shall separate me from the love of Christ." Then he also sang, "Though an army should set itself in array against me, my heart shall not be afraid." Then the enemy, who despises good, astonished that even after the blows he had received, he dared to return, summoned his dogs and said, exploding with rage, "You see that we failed to stop this man with a spirit of fornication or with lashes. Far from it—he is even insolent to us. Let us approach him in another way." Now schemes for working evil come easily to the devil, so when it was nighttime, they made such a crashing noise that the whole place seemed to be shaken by a quake. The demons, as if breaking through the building's four walls, and seeming to enter through them, were changed into the forms of beasts and reptiles.[12]

Bravely facing these frightening forces, Anthony was finally delivered when a beam of light seemed to descend from the ceiling. Instantly, the attacks ceased and his suffering was relieved; he felt stronger than ever before.

This is a good model for the Christian tradition: neither running from fearful experiences nor indulging pleasant ones. Rather, we simply return to our practice, leaving everything else behind. The author of *The Cloud of Unknowing* writes:

And so you may confidently rely on this gentle stirring of love in your heart and follow wherever it leads you, for it is your sure guide in this life and will bring you to the glory of the next....The delight and consolations of sense and spirit, regardless how sublime, are but accidental to this and wholly dependent on it....[13]

Some people experience a measure of consolation almost always, while others only rarely. But God, in his great wisdom, determines what is best for each one....[14]

Chapter 4

Happiness
and Salvation

We have two different ideas of happiness and salvation. Somehow they belong together, but in searching for word associations, we come up with two very different meanings. Happiness connotes pleasant experiences often relating to food, home, shelter, and the satisfaction of physical needs. We also associate certain emotional comforts with happiness: acceptance, affection, security, and status. We do not associate anxiety, suffering, conflict, loneliness, or death with happiness.

When we speak of salvation, we think of something much broader than happiness. Embracing salvation means we have found a satisfactory answer to the question "What is the meaning of life?"

Although the paths to salvation are many—and generally religious paths—they all have one thing in common. They lead through confrontation and suffering, through anguish, anxiety, death, and dying. In the Christian tradition, the life of Jesus, which we commemorate throughout the year, reveals this path to us and allows us to accompany him through all the stages of salvation from birth to Mount Tabor, from Golgotha to the Resurrection. Reflecting on Jesus' life, we can conclude that happiness and salvation can well contradict each other.

The road to salvation is not a broad thoroughfare. It passes through a narrow gate, follows a narrow path, and takes us through the depths of the unconscious where we are confronted with people, the world, the devil, death, and God. Mysticism gives this part of the journey the name "Purgative Way." Very often, we can do nothing during this passage except suffer the situation. During this time, it is important to accept the suffering not as a tragedy, but as a process of transformation.

The journey through midlife gives us an opportunity to accept suffering that is transformative. Generally, between the ages of thirty and forty, we are confronted with the question of life's meaning. Prior to this time, we are outwardly oriented. We project our expectations of salvation onto the outside world. The search for a partner, sexual satisfaction, power, money, profession, and career achievements conceals our deeper yearning for meaning and a conclusive fulfillment in life.

Jung understood human nature very well when he said that human religious longing is a more compelling force than either sexuality or power.

Amongst all my patients on the far side of middle age—that is to say, over thirty five—there is not one whose fundamental problem does not rest with his religious adjustment. Each and every one suffer finally from the fact that he has lost what every living religion throughout the ages has given its believers. And not one is really healed who hasn't recovered his religious focus, which has nothing to do with denominations or membership in a particular church.

Salvation and Psychotherapy

Many therapists are concerned only with people's happiness. Their goal is to help people deal with their daily lives while experiencing a minimum of suffering and tension. Some therapists, however, recognize a spiritual dimension as an integral element of the healing process.

Therapists who acknowledge the spiritual dimension recognize that there are many people with a "noogenic" neuroses, or metapathology as Abraham Maslow terms it. (A noogenic neurosis comes from suppressing spiritual needs, which leads to symptoms similar to those found in the suppression of other needs). At times, such symptoms can indicate genuine mental illness requiring specialized therapy. Sometimes, however, the state of transformation during contemplation is misunderstood and classified as a psychopathic illness when, in fact, a true transformative process is underway. In contemplation, psychological suffering often has a much deeper meaning. It signals a radical change, a new sense of direction in one's view of life.

Unfortunately, transpersonal experiences mean nothing to many therapists. In their academic way of thinking, there is no category for them to file things transpersonal. Still widely accepted is Freud's reaction to a friend's letter in which his friend described a mystical experience. Freud said at that time that he looked into himself but found no similar experience. Therefore, in his opinion, it would probably be best to categorize it within the psychoanalytical framework.

Other psychotherapists, such as Viktor Frankl or Carl Jung, are convinced that help for people suffering this way comes from belief in an ultimate truth. Whether the person holds to a specific faith and calls this truth God, or experiences this truth as a power that gives meaning to life, is secondary.

Access to the deeper layers of the psyche may have something to do with religious experience. We call these experiences transpersonal. Psychoanalysis may gain access to the spiritual dimension by preparing individuals for the transpersonal sphere.

Contemplation: A Critical Look at the Meaning of Life

A very important task of midlife is coming to terms with the reality of our own physical death. As with any other suppressed aspects of reality, failing to integrate our physical mortality into awareness has detrimental psychological effects. Meeting this challenge liberates us from the binding fear of death and frees us to live life fully.

When we die, we do not have the sense of life coming to an end; rather, life goes on. In out-of-body experiences during instances of near-death, there appears to be a comprehension and awareness beyond our day-to-day consciousness, beyond intellectual and sensory perception. What we experience then is what esoterics often call our astral body. We Christians use the word *soul*, although both expressions do not necessarily mean the same thing. At death, we leave our bodies and experience a separation of our essential identity from our physical reality, which no longer concerns us.

Contemplation: Learning to Die

Contemplation is a matter of learning to surrender, learning to let go. Much depends on whether we are ready to accept a new sphere of existence or whether we cling to this one.

Through research, thanatologists have mapped the stages of dying. These phases include a feeling of lightness and joy at being freed from restrictive physical conditions (often accompanied with an aversion to reenter the physical body). These phases also involve movement through a dark tunnel, at the end of which appears a bright light, a luminous Being who greets the person, and a review of one's entire life, as in a reel of film. There is no judge, only unimaginable self-knowledge. In the case of death by accident, one stands in the face of death, but decides to return to the physical body, realizing that there are yet unfinished life tasks that need attention. This may happen if one has not recognized the meaning of life and lived accordingly, if one has been dominated by an egocentric concept and attitude toward life, or if one's interest in spiritual evolution has remained underdeveloped.

It appears that each of us must take up in the next life where we leave off in this one. Someone who was about to commit suicide by jumping from the tenth floor suddenly recognized this fact: "I can jump, I can die, but all my unsolved problems will accompany me into my next life to be solved there."

Of course, the way we die is dependent upon the way we live. Naturally, we all hope to be clarified in the meeting with the loving Reality. But chances are that each of us will behave in the new existence similarly to the way we behave in this one, since the orientation which guides us in this life will accompany us into the next.

In everyday existence, we project an environment similar to what we do when we dream. When we're in the dream environment, we don't stop to question reality; we believe that the dream environment is real. The same is true after death; we live a new existence which we experience according to the capacity of our awareness. It will be a dimension that we find as real as the present existence or the world of our dreams.

Christians believe in future forms of life. We call one of these forms "purgatory," an existence in which the process of our purification and perfection continues. We also believe in two other dimensions of life: heaven and hell. I believe that between our life here and our final existence there may be many other phases where we have the opportunity to mature into the complete *imago Dei*. We must learn, however, to surrender and let go of the desire to make any dimension our final home.

Life often presents us with situations in which we do not know what to do. We will not fail if we respond in love, since love is the way to God. Saint Augustine said, "Love and do what you will." The love that exists between human beings points the way to Ultimate Reality.

It must be said again, however, that we cannot simply change our orientation at will; it is more a question of an inner transformation. It is not we who change ourselves but, in truth, it is the Divine unfolding within us. Letting go means letting God be God in us. The mystics refer to this as passive purification. Transformation and purification are marked by phases of suffering and confusion during which one experiences various spiritual and emotional stages, and even somatic changes.

Ego-Awareness and Universal Consciousness

If we take the path of contemplation, we discover that our ego-awareness is but an instrument of our total awareness. Ego-awareness is the great hypnotizer, dangling before us an illusion of reality. In India, they refer to this as the great Magician Maya, who conjures up all things only to let them flounder and disappear. We must learn that this, our ego, is not our true identity. Our true identity, which we are seeking in contemplation and which will accompany us after death, is much deeper.

Life, therefore, is not identical with the ego. Our real existence is divine Life, which is like a spring that brings forth all these various forms. Only those who experience this spring, this Life itself, can experience their own true identity.

A twig that experiences itself as a twig on a tree and sees the other twigs, trunk, and roots is comparable to our ego-awareness or ego. That is knowledge stemming from intellectual and sensory perception. But the twig can also experience itself from within; it experiences itself as a tree. That doesn't mean it stops being a twig, but it is in union with all that makes up the tree. It is one with the trunk, with the roots, and with the other branches. To experience ourselves from within, as the twig experiences itself as tree: this is our goal. To experience this oneness is not to abolish differentiation.

It must be said yet again, however, that this ego that we must leave behind is not a negative thing. It is that which makes us human. It is part of a coordinated system, supernatural and natural, divine and human, spiritual and material. The ego has the tendency to elude every change—and this, too, is not negative. It tries to keep things stable, thus giving birth to the drama of human conflict and human history. It forms cultures and defies all change, creating a tension between preserving the old and allowing the new to emerge. The ego does not have to die, but become transparent.

Chapter 5

Contemporary Considerations in Contemplation

C hristian mystical writers use the word *contemplation* in reference to a specific kind of objectless prayer. The Victorine mystics, for example, distinguished three levels of knowledge of God. Hugh of Saint Victor writes of thinking (cogitatio), meditation (meditatio), and contemplation (contemplatio). Thinking and meditation, he writes, can give us indirect knowledge of God via objects of sense and intellect. But in contemplation there is no such object; rather, the soul is united directly with God in an act of intuitive insight.

Saint Bonaventure, following in the footsteps of the Victorines, distinguished three types of knowledge obtained by the "eye of the flesh," the "eye of reason," and the "eye of contemplation." In his book *Eye to Eye,* Ken Wilber presents Bonaventure's thesis.

St. Bonaventure, the great *Doctor Seraphicus* of the Church and a favorite philosopher of Western mystics, taught that men and women have at least three modes of attaining knowledge—"three eyes," as he put it: the *eye of flesh,* by which we perceive the external world of space, time, and objects; the *eye of reason,* by which we attain a knowledge of philosophy, logic, and the mind itself; and the *eye of contemplation,* by which we rise to a knowledge of transcendent realities.

Further, said St. Bonaventure, all knowledge is a type of *illumination.* There is exterior and inferior illumination, which lights the eye of flesh and gives us knowledge of sense objects. There is interior illumination, which lights the eye of reason and gives us knowledge of philosophical truth. And there is superior illumination, the light of transcendent Being which illumines the eye of contemplation and reveals salutary truth, "truth which is unto liberation."

In the external world, said St. Bonaventure, we find a "vestige of God"—and the eye of flesh perceives this vestige (which appears as separate objects in space and time). In ourselves, in our psyches—especially in the "threefold activity of the soul" (memory, reason, and will)—we find an *imago* of God, revealed by the mental eye. And ultimately, through the eye of contemplation, lighted by the superior illumination, we find the whole transcendent realm itself, beyond sense and reason—the Divine Ultimate itself.

Now that particular wording, eye of flesh, mind, and contemplation—is Christian; but similar ideas can be found in every major school of traditional psychology, philosophy, and religion. The "three eyes" of a human being correspond, in fact, to the three major realms of being described by the perennial philosophy, which are the gross (flesh and material), the subtle (mental and animic), and the causal (transcendent and contemplative).[1]

In other words, writes Wilber, Christianity (as well as Buddhism and other great religions) has, from its origin, contained direct insights into Ultimate Reality. The problem was that these insights

were invariably all mixed up with rational truths and empirical facts. Humanity had not, as it were, yet learned to differentiate and separate the eyes of flesh, reason, and contemplation. And because Revelation was confused with logic and with empirical fact, and all three were presented as *one truth*, then two things happened: the philosophers came in and destroyed the rational side of religion, and science came in and destroyed the empirical side. I will argue that that was as it should be. However, theology—which in the West had a somewhat weak eye of contemplation anyway—was so heavily dependent upon its rationalism and empirical "facts" (the sun circles the earth as the Bible says), that when these two eyes were taken away by philosophy and science, Western spirituality all but went blind. It did not fall back on its eye of contemplation—but merely fell apart and spent its time in futile argument with the philosophers and scientists. From that point on, spirituality in the West was dismantled, and only philosophy and science seriously remained.

Within a century, however, philosophy as a rational system—a system based on the eye of mind—was in its own turn decimated, and decimated by the new scientific empiricism. At that point, human knowledge was *reduced* to only the eye of flesh. Gone was the contemplative eye; gone the mental eye—and human beings had enough collective low self-esteem to restrict their means of valid knowledge to the eye of flesh—the eye we share with animals. Knowing became, in source and referent, essentially subhuman.[2]

Kataphatic and Apophatic Spirituality

The problem, as outlined by Wilber, arose in part because of Christianity's confusion of two spiritual paths to God. The theological terms for these paths are *kataphatic* and *apophatic*. The kataphatic path (from the Greek *kata* meaning "into" or "toward," and *oatis* meaning "word") is a conceptual path; the apophatic path (from the Greek *apo* meaning "away from") is free of all concepts. These two paths are found in all major world religions.

Kataphatic spirituality deals with the contents of consciousness: images, symbols, and ideas. A variety of conceptualizations plays a primary role along this way. Apophatic spirituality, on the other hand, is oriented toward pure, empty consciousness. Any content to this consciousness is thus an obstacle. As long as the mind is engaged with images or conceptualization, any direct experience of God is impossible.

Most people live their religious lives on the kataphatic path. Kataphatic spirituality certainly plays the larger role in every world religion today. Even in Hinduism and Buddhism—religions with ancient and highly developed apophatic traditions—

few devotees resolutely take the apophatic paths. Hinduism, for example, has many highly ornate images of God. Japanese Buddhists, in great numbers, venerate Amida Buddha, as well as Kannon and Jizo, two popular objects of Bodhisattva veneration. Even Tibetan Buddhism uses visualizations, though these are intended to lead one finally onto the apophatic path.

Concepts, dogma, and other devices can also veil our image of God, yet they are only windows through which we view Ultimate Reality. Such windows may be triangular, rectangular, or round, but we make a tragic mistake if we conclude that *God* is a square or a triangle or a circle.

There is, of course, nothing wrong with any of these kataphatic ways because religious experience cannot be communicated apart from images and symbols. Without these devices, organized religion would simply not exist. But it is essential to see the limits of these linguistic and conceptual devices, for they are only "fingers pointing toward the moon"; we must not mistake them for the moon itself. It is crucial that we see through all such devices and experience the God who is beyond the grasp of them all.

And so Moses, when he asked, was given no name for God. All that he could take back to the Israelites was the expression, "I AM WHO I AM" (Exodus 3:14). For most of the Israelites, however, this simply was not enough, and they erected the golden calf. We, too, even after a direct experience of Being, tend to immediately begin clouding it with our own conceptualization. Such is the nature of the intellect. The apophatic way is a way of constantly letting go of all such mental maneuverings, all devices that limit the infinite expanse of the Ultimate Reality.

Because the apophatic path is a "via negativa," a way of unknowing, apophatic theology and language contain as much negative imagery as positive statements. We have considered John of the Cross' *nada, nada, nada,* and Eckhart writes, "So be silent and do not chatter about God, because by chattering about him you are lying and committing a sin."[3] So, too, the author of *The Cloud of Unknowing* and most other classic mystical texts resort, finally, to saying what God is *not*—and then pointing to the provisional nature of even *these* statements.

Certainly there is a danger here. Apophatic spirituality has always been considered somewhat suspect in Christianity, and at times this mistrust has been justified. Movements within the apophatic tradition have been known to become strongly anti-theological, anti-intellectual and even parapsychical. Disregarding a constructively critical attitude, they have abused the authority and responsibility they had to lead people into transmental experience.

In the final analysis, the kataphatic and apophatic traditions depend on, complement, and instruct each other. They are like two strong pillars and only beneath their roof may a healthy, balanced religious life exist and flourish.

Ego and Self

Mystics distinguish between what we call the "ego" and the "true self." The ego is the intersection where the various interests of the intellect, emotions, perception, memory, and will meet. What we commonly refer to as "I" is the point at which these powers intersect and simulate the conviction that this ego is an enduring, separate entity. In fact, however, this is not so, and understanding the nature of this simulation—seeing through this trick of awareness—is a crucial step along the contemplative path.

As long as our attention is engaged on the ego level, our true self—our essential nature—is obscured. It is as if sediment has been stirred up in a pond and the water made muddy; we cannot peer into the depths of the pond. Likewise, only when the ego becomes quiet, its various powers completely still, can we behold the depths of our own being. There we experience that which we have been from the beginning, our true self. Eckhart calls this "the spark of the soul"; Tauler calls it "the Ground"; Teresa of Avila calls it "the Interior Castle." It is the same reality the gospels speak of: the kingdom of God, the kingdom of heaven, and eternal life.

Clearly, therefore, it is important to let go of all concepts and images of God. Helpful though they may be, they do engage our attention at the ego level and stand as obstacles to our experience of who we really are. In his book *Will and Spirit*, Gerald May suggests that the production of thoughts and images during contemplation is a device ego-consciousness uses to protect itself from abandonment. Any image or idea, in other words, presupposes an "I" standing in opposite from it. And it is precisely this "I" that must become transparent along the contemplative path.

While much contemplative literature mentions the necessity of the death of the ego, it is wrong to conclude that the ego itself is inherently evil. It is only our exclusive identification with this level of awareness that constitutes "sin." Once we have transcended this level of awareness and experienced the whole of our being, the ego begins to turn transparent, and the light of our essential nature shines through.

God: The Essence of Being

From earliest times, Christian dogma has been based on a very definite model of the universe. Since the time of Galileo, however, the Church has had difficulties because of this conception—and continues to have them today. While Christian theology is constantly evolving, its perspective on the universe is, in essence, exactly as it was at Galileo's time. According to this prevailing view, God is the creator of the universe and the center of the universe is earth. God's attention, as it were, is likewise centered on this planet and its inhabitants. Christianity has constructed a whole salvation drama based on these assumptions—a drama that begins with the creation story and humanity's "fall" from grace, moves to the birth and death of Jesus, and is projected into the future and Christ's return.

But human knowledge now recognizes that this earth is but a small planet in a macrocosmos of unfathomable numbers of solar systems and galaxies, some quite like our own and probably inhabited by intelligent life. Thus, it is simply no longer helpful to use this model as a point of departure from which to interpret God and salvation.

One of the major drawbacks of this prevailing view is the assumption that God and humanity are deeply separated. God has become so far removed from creation that the two are considered entirely different orders: creation is "natural," and God is "supernatural." The gap between these two can never be bridged, even in what is called "heaven." At the same time, according to this view, there is a "hell," a part of creation that will always and forever be separate from God. This entire view is deeply dualistic; it breaks down the cosmos into opposing camps: the natural and the supernatural, the creator and the created, the good and the evil, the saved and the damned.

And yet another model of existence has always been available to humanity, a model that, since the time of the German philosopher Leibnitz, has been called *philosophia perennis*. This view of the cosmos parallels that found in many Eastern religions. First promulgated in the West by the pre-Socratics, it was enlarged upon by various philosophers and mystics ranging from Parmenides, who inaugurated Western metaphysical thinking, and Plotinus, a great philosopher and religious genius of the third century A.D., to Eckhart and John of the Cross. *Philosophia perennis* is based in a transscientific understanding of the universe. It posits the existence of an Ultimate Reality or Absolute—"the Godhead," as Eckhart would say—that is the essence of all that is. This view understands that while this Reality is the origin of the universe, it is not a creator set apart from what is created. Rather, in this view, God is the origin of all things, indwells within them, and is their deepest identity.

To explain it further, Eckhart says that the difference between God and man is the difference between giving birth and being born. But giving birth and being born is of one essence—just as the source and stream are of one water. Thomas Aquinas wrote that God is *Natura Naturans*—both the form of life and life itself. The Gospel of John quotes Jesus saying the same thing: "The glory that you have given me I have given them, so that they may be one, as we are one" (17:22).

No one has ever seen life apart from the forms it animates. We see people, not "human life"; trees, not "arboreal existence." Thus, we perceive the formless only through form—or better, only *as* form itself. The physical world, human beings, and everything that is are all forms of the Ultimate Reality, all expressions of God, all "one with the Father."

Viewing the cosmos in this way, our understanding of religion is bound to be transformed as well. Once we stop anthropomorphizing God, in however subtle ways, as a being set apart from ourselves and all that is, religion may still constitute a pathway to salvation. Our understanding of salvation itself, however, will have changed. Salvation will now be nothing other than a realization of the fact that "the kingdom of God is within you"; this simple *seeing* of things as they really are will constitute our beatific vision.

This is the Good News Jesus proclaimed to humanity. The kingdom is already within all of us, quite literally, nearer to us than we can imagine. "Today this scripture has been fulfilled in your hearing" (Luke 4:21).

Incarnation

If the whole of creation is an expression of the Divine, incarnation did not begin nor end with Jesus Christ. Incarnation *has always been* the case. It will always be so. Apart from incarnation, nothing exists: "All things came into being through him, and without him not one thing came into being" (John 1:3).

Jesus Christ is a *typus*—a "type"—in which all existence is summarized. The whole of reality flashed forth in his person, nondualistic, one. In him, the Divine revealed its phenomenal aspect—God "became flesh and dwelt among us." And this is precisely what happens in the case of each of us. The whole thrust of Jesus' life, the essential content of the gospel message, is a calling for our realization of this fact.

Christian art often portrays this coincidence of the human and the Divine in the person of Jesus Christ. In both the East and the West, the mandorla, comprised of two intersecting circles, portrays the relationship between these two aspects of reality—the spiritual and the material, heaven and earth, the human and the divine.

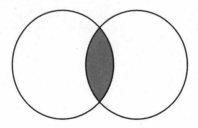

In its earliest form, the mandorla placed the circle representing the Divine above the circle representing the worldly; later, the two were placed side by side. Both of these arrangements are in evidence throughout Christian art. Nicholas of Cusa called this symbolic arrangement the "coincidence of opposites"—the bipolar unity of reality. This place, according to Nicholas, is where one may find God unveiled. It is surrounded by the coincidence of opposites. This is the wall of the paradise in which God resides. Its gate is guarded by the rational mind. If one does not overpower the rational mind, the entrance will not open. Beyond the wall of the coincidence of opposites, one is able to see God; on this side, however, one cannot see God.

We may view the process of human maturation as a bringing together of these two circles until we experience the inherent oneness. Our ego-awareness obscures this essential unity. The Gospel of John speaks of this unity: "Whoever has seen me has seen the Father" and "Do you not believe that I am in the Father and the Father is in me?" (14:9-10). Certain apocryphal texts are even more pointed. In the Gospel of Thomas we read: "When you have turned two into one you will become sons of man." And again,

> When you turn two into one, and when you make the inner like the outer, the outer like the inner and the above like the below, and when you turn the feminine and the masculine into a unity so that the masculine is not masculine and the feminine is not feminine, then you will enter the kingdom.[4]

Another symbol of oneness is the Star of David, which originated in central Asia.

Like the two circles of the mandorla, the two triangles of the Star share a common area. Ideally, these two triangles—representing the two aspects of reality—will rotate against each other until they merge into a single triangle, one reality.

The cross, common to both East and West, is the oldest such symbol of any known religion:

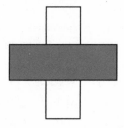

The horizontal and vertical axes of the cross represent the two aspects of reality: the human and the Divine. Alone, neither aspect makes a complete person; both are part of the whole. We can lose our way in the spiritual as well as in the material realm. The truly human standpoint is that at which these two axes intersect, as they do in the person of Jesus. In him, both aspects are integrated: God is personalized, and the divine Life is fully and consciously incarnate.

Accordingly, Christ is a *symbolon,* a sign of recognition, in which we realize what we really are from the beginning. (*Symbolon* is a Greek word meaning "that which has been put together." A symbolon might be an earthen vessel broken by friends. When a messenger brought one half from one friend to the other—who fit it perfectly with its mate—the authenticity of the message was confirmed.) When Jesus was born, God "came to what was his own," reads the Gospel of John 1:11). The divine Life awakened within a human personality—and the symbolon was joined perfectly. This absolute coincidence of the human and the Divine in the person of Jesus is the true message of the gospels. When Meister Eckhart wonders why we raise up Christ and revere him as our Lord and God, he exercises the symbolon in his explanation: because Christ was God's messenger to us and brought us our blessedness. The blessedness he brought us was our own.

Therefore, observes Saint Paul, we must not only hear this message and believe it, we must come to embody it, so that "it is no longer I who live, but it is Christ who lives in me" (Galatians 2:20). He urges the Colossians to strip "off the old self with its practices and…cloth[ed] yourselves with the new self" (3:9-10).

But how do we put off the old nature? We let go of our exclusive identification with our ego minds, with but half of the mandorla. Only then may we come to realize that we are from the beginning clothed in the new, that the small "I" has never lived at all, but only Christ, only the divine Life, exists and animates all things.

Mind and Matter

In recent years, physicists have begun talking about the universe in terms remarkably like those used by the ancient apophatic traditions. In Zen Buddhism, for instance, mind and matter are considered two aspects of the same reality. And while Newtonian physics separated energy and matter and considered them essentially different things, physicists today generally concur with the Zen view: these two are really only organizational forms of a single reality.

Albert Einstein called matter "concentrated energy," pointing out that either can be transformed into the other. The German physicist Max Planck explains that there is no such thing as matter, that creation and existence of all matter lies solely in a force which sets the atomic particles in motion and holds them together in the form of tiny solar systems or atoms.

In more recent years, a number of particles more elementary even than atoms have been discovered. "Quarks" and other mysterious particles change into force fields and appear and disappear—and no one is quite sure where they come from or where they go.

As science widens the circumference of its knowledge, it comes more and more frequently into contact with what has traditionally been the realm of philosophers and mystics. The more empirical data we amass, the more aware we become of the limitations of empirical knowledge. As marvelous as the human intellect is, it becomes increasingly apparent that intellectual inquiry will never grasp the whole of reality. It is as if the intellect itself is a borderline: as it extends itself, so, too, our awareness of what lies beyond it is extended. Thus, we have such eminent scientists as Einstein stating that

> The most beautiful emotion we can experience is the mystical. It is the sower of all true art and science. He to whom this emotion is a stranger...is as good as dead. To know that what is impenetrable to us really exists, manifesting itself as the highest wisdom and the most radiant beauty, which our dull faculties can comprehend only in their most primitive forms—this knowledge, this feeling, is at the center of true religiousness. In this sense,

and in this sense only, I belong to the ranks of devoutly religious men.[5]

Even as modern physics moves inexorably toward a more comprehensive model of the universe, psychology and the other life sciences increasingly find their inquiries probing the transpersonal realm. Nobel prize winner Eccles and other researchers of the human brain report that our mind constructs such things as mathematical equations only by receiving, piecing together, and interpreting frequencies from a dimension beyond space and time. In his book *The Doors of Perception and Heaven and Hell*, Aldous Huxley reflects on such theories after he experienced a dramatic opening of his own mind.

Reflecting on my experience, I find myself agreeing with the eminent Cambridge philosopher, Dr. C.D. Broad, "that we should do well to consider much more seriously...the type of theory which Bergson put forward in connection with memory and sense perception. The suggestion is that the function of the brain and nervous system and sense organs is in the main eliminative and not productive. Each person is at each moment capable of remembering all that has ever happened to him and of perceiving everything that is happening everywhere in the universe. The function of the brain and nervous system is to protect us from being overwhelmed and confused by this mass of largely useless and irrelevant knowledge, by shutting out most of what we should otherwise perceive or remember at any moment, and leaving only that very small and special selection which is likely to be practically useful.

According to such a theory, each one of us is potentially Mind At Large. But in so far as we are animals, our business is at all costs to survive. To make biological survival possible, Mind At Large has to be funneled through the reducing valve of the brain and nervous system. What comes out at the other end is a measly trickle of the kind of consciousness which will help us to stay alive on the surface of this particular planet....Most people, most of the time, know only what comes through the reducing valve and is consecrated as genuinely real by the local language. Certain persons, however, seem to be born with a kind of bypass that circumvents the reducing valve. In others, temporary bypasses may be acquired either spontaneously or as the result of deliberate "spiritual exercises" or through hypnosis or by means of drugs. Through these permanent or temporary bypasses there flows, not indeed the perception "of everything that is happening everywhere in the universe" (for the bypass does not abolish the reducing valve, which still excludes the total content of Mind At Large), but something more than, and above all something different from, the carefully selected utilitarian material which our narrowed, individual minds regard as a complete, or at least sufficient, picture of reality.[6]

It seems safe to conclude that this Mind at Large, the origin of matter and, in fact, matter itself, is none other than what the Christian contemplative path calls "God." Just as H_2O can exists in various forms—ice, water, steam—so this Mind expresses itself in different ways. Our individual consciousness is one expression of it. Jaensch, an experimental psychologist best known for his work on eidetic imagery, writes, "God is the mind of the universe." Indeed, God is the organizational principle, the dynamic of all that exists. Saint Paul's admonition to put on the mind of Christ is a call to realize this fact, to awaken to the true nature of ourselves and of all things.

Time and Space

Based on our observation of motion, we posit the existence of time and space. But beyond this observation, beyond our conclusions regarding it—or better, before these things—there is only the present moment, quite free of temporal or spatial limitations. Christianity calls this eternal present "eternity."

Frequently the term *eternity* is understood in terms of yesterday and tomorrow, an infinite progression of time in two directions. But this is a misunderstanding. Eternity is our native condition, the essentially timeless fact of our existence. While it is the environment in which our intellectual activities and sense perceptions arise, it is beyond the grasp of either.

When we realize this fundamental context for our lives, we must then reconsider many articles of our religious faith. For example, the Resurrection is not something that will happen in some future context. At this very moment, we *are* resurrected and dwelling in heaven. To realize this fact, we need only let go of our ideas about life and death, past, and future; life and death are only concepts, mere side effects of the eternal now. This complete letting go is itself our resurrection.

Prophecy is but one phenomenon that gives rise to the lie about our usual conception of the existence of time and the fixed course it runs. Fortunately, there are and have been, within and without each great religious tradition, individuals capable of recognizing and relating events placed throughout the continuum of time—past, present, and future. Similarly, various phenomena demonstrate that our fixed ideas about space and matter are entirely too rigid to encompass physical reality. At transmental levels of awareness, it becomes clear that individual objects are not intrinsically separate from the field from which they arise—the Mind at Large or God. Rather, these things are only manifestations of this one reality.

My Beloved Is the Mountains

We can distinguish between two kinds of mystical experience. In the first, we experience ourself becoming one with all things. Our awareness, until then limited to sense experience, broadens, and we recognize the common life that animates all that is. As one woman's account of her experience states:

> I took a walk and stopped in front of a tree that stood by the wayside. Suddenly everything was different. The boundaries between myself and the tree had disappeared. I was the tree, too. Everything was very real and clear; a very great joy arose from within me. But it was not the joy about some special or specific thing. Rather, it was the joy at realizing that everything was the way it was and that everything was all right the way it was. It was a religious experience although I didn't think of God at all.

In the second kind of mystical experience, we realize complete, undifferentiated unity. Unlike the first kind of experience, in which a common life is perceived in all things, the second experience is only aware of divine Being itself. Intellectual and empirical elements are excluded, time and space no longer exist. There is no self to experience or be experienced. There is only God.

It seems that John of the Cross was describing this ultimate experience of unity when he wrote in *The Spiritual Canticle*:

My Beloved is the mountains,
And lonely wooded valleys,
Strange islands,
And resounding rivers,
The whistling of love-stirring breezes,

The tranquil night
At the time of the rising dawn,
Silent music,
Sounding solitude,
The supper that refreshes, and deepens love.[7]

In his interpretation of these verses, John writes:

The Beloved is all these things in Himself, and that He is so also for (the soul), because in such superabundant communications from God, the soul experiences and knows the truth of St. Francis' prayer: *My God and my all.*

It should be known that what is explained here is present in God eminently and infinitely, or better, each of these sublime attributes is God, and all of them together are God.

Inasmuch as the soul in this case is united with God, she feels that all things are God.[8]

Once we mature to a certain point in our contemplative practice, a breakthrough into transmental awareness can be triggered by literally anything at all. From the East come enlightenment stories of how a cherry blossom, the cry of a bird, or the sound of a stone striking bamboo can open the mind of those who are maturing along the contemplative path. From the Christian tradition come similar stories: Elias, for example, who experienced God in the whistling sound of a light breeze. John of the Cross writes:

This divine whistling which enters through the soul's hearing is not only, as I have said, the understood substance, but also an unveiling of truths about the divinity and a revelation of His secrets.[9]

Saint Paul, too, on the road to Damascus, "heard things which cannot be put into words—things that human lips may not speak." John of the Cross concludes, "It is thought that he saw God there as our Father Elias also did in the whistling."[10]

In addition to various external stimuli, a concept or emotion can also trigger transmental experience. Something like this seems to have occurred to Teresa of Avila and John of the Cross as they conversed about the Blessed Trinity. Both shared a deep mystical experience. The religious content of their discussion was quite incidental to the experience itself. John also seems to have come into transmental experience upon hearing a young man in the street playing his guitar and singing a love song to his girlfriend.

The verbal expression of transmental experience has posed a challenge to mystics of all religions and every age. A contemplative woman living today wrote in an account of her experience, "While taking a walk, I heard a man laugh in his garden. He laughed the Great Name." Here, the woman breaks off her narrative to observe, "But it can't be the way I said it." Immediately her rational mind began censoring what, in fact, was a very accurate description of her experience.

Perhaps this kind of censoring is inevitable. Human language is simply not equipped to express mystical experience in a way that satisfies both the speaker and the listener. As a result, mystics often resort to poetry, to negative statements, or to silence, which, as Eckhart said, is the most beautiful thing anyone can say about God. Jesus often used stories and images to communicate his experience, and so have many others. Tolstoi noted that Christ teaches that there is something within humankind that elevates it beyond this life with its haste, its anxiety, its lust. He says that whoever grasps the teaching of Christ experiences the same feeling as that of a bird that did not know it possessed wings but gradually came to understand that it could fly, that it could be free, that it did not need to fear anything.

"The same feeling as that of a bird"; "It is like a mustard seed"; "My Beloved is the mountains"; "He laughed the Great Name." These are the follies into which human language slips when it attempts to communicate what is, essentially, transverbal experience. Accordingly, such experience is often labeled Pantheism, Gnosticism, or Monism. But such classifications describe forms of cognition that begin and end in the intellect. Perhaps, from a purely intellectual standpoint, certain statements of the mystics correspond to the intellectual formulations of the Pantheist or the Monist. But the one who has personally entered into transmental experience knows that the mystic speaks of a way of knowing that has nothing to do with the intellect.

Afterword

What is the meaning of existence? What is the meaning of a tree, an animal, a human being? Eckhart would have said that they exist "beyond question." And Angelus Silesius wrote: "The rose does have no why; it blossoms without reason, forgetful of itself; oblivious to our vision."[1]

Why are we on the earth? That was the first question I learned from the old catechism. The answer was: "To know, love, and serve God here and to be happy with Him hereafter." I still ascribe to that today. Yet, my understanding of it has matured.

Life, which we may call God, the Absolute, the Ultimate Reality, True Being, and so forth, permeates and expresses Self in everything. This True Being is the heart of our existence. God is the Being out of which we live; God is the Being that lives in us and through us. We are God's form of expression.

Our ego-consciousness hinders us from experiencing our essential nature. We don't know who we are, and we cannot define who we are. We can only experience it. Our ego-consciousness cuts us off only from the experience, not from Being. Yet, the unmediated experience of our Essential Nature has a profound influence in our daily lives, an influence that cannot be fully realized through philosophy, theology, ritual, or sacrament alone.

When mystics speak of the Divine in human beings, they sometimes say, "I am God." Unfortunately, that is easily misunderstood as pantheism. Yet, the mystic doesn't stop being human; the mystic merely "realizes his [her] coincidence with God" as represented in the mandorla. Where Christian mysticism is not pressed through a dogmatic sieve, it expresses this as clearly as Eastern mysticism. In *The Living Flame of Love*, John of the Cross wrote, "Our awakening is an awakening of God and our rising (from the dead) is God's rising (from the dead)."[2]

Ultimate Reality—God—knows neither inside nor outside. The wave does not exist apart from the ocean. The wave is the ocean, but it is also not the ocean. Eastern mysticism uses the expression "not-two." The individual existential form does not vanish in the experience of God. The mystic experiences this form of existence as the form of God. The wave experiences itself as ocean. It is, indeed, the realization of what Tauler called "the Ground," Eckhart called "Godhead," Teresa called "the Interior Castle," and Zen called "Essential Nature."

Spiritual life is not synonymous with subjugation to moral regulations, dogmas, or rituals. It is what Eckhart means when he says that we should get out of God's way so that God can be God in us.

God alone is reality—ever-present—permeating everything and expressing Self in everything. There is no form of life that is more holy than any other. Everything is the symphony of God, the dance of God the dancer.

The esoteric paths of the great religions teach practices that lead to quieting of the ego-consciousness, so that we are able to experience Universal Consciousness. This is the divine Consciousness; "God is known by God"[3] "so his knowing is mine,"[4] "God's ground is my ground" and "the eye with which I see God is the same eye with which God sees me."[5]

Notes

Chapter 1:
The Source and Goal of Religion

1. Ken Wilber, *Eye to Eye: The Quest for the New Paradigm* (Garden City, NY: Anchor Press, 1983). The following is an adaptation of the Chapter: "Development, Meditation, and the Unconscious."
2. Josef Quint, *Meister Eckhart: Deutsche Predigen und Traktate* (München, Germany: Carl Hanser Verlag, 1978), 29
3. M. O'C. Walshe, Translator, *Meister Eckhart: Sermons and Treatises* (London, England: Watkins Publishing, 1979), I: 117.

4. R. Blakney, Translator, *Meister Eckhart* (New York, NY: Harper and Row Publishers, 1941), 245.

5. Quint, *Meister Eckhart: Deutsche Predigen und Traktate*, 353-355.

6. K. Kavanaugh and O. Rodriquez, Translators, *The Collected Works of St. John of the Cross* (Washington, D.C: Institute of Carmelite Studies Publication, 1979). All citations are from this edition. *The Ascent Of Mount Carmel*, III, 12, 1.

7. Ibid., 11, 1.

8. Ibid., 12, 2.

9. Kavanaugh, *The Living Flame of Love*, 4,9.

10. Abbot Zenkei Shibayama, *A Flower Does Not Talk* (Rutland, VT: Charles Tuttle Company, 1980), 95-96.

11. Blakeny, *Meister Eckhart*, 238

12. Walshe, *Meister Eckhart: Sermons and Treatises*, I, 150.

13. Ibid., 88.

14. Kōun Yamada, *Gateless Gate* (Tucson, AZ: University of Arizona Press, 1990), 212

15. Blakney, *Meister Eckhart*, 9.

16. This story is quoted in *Yin Und Yang*, Suakie Colegrave; Otto Wilhelm Barth Verlag.

17. Blakney, *Meister Eckhart*, 199.

18. Walshe, *Meister Eckhart: Sermons and Treatises*, I, 34.

Chapter 2:
The Practice of Contemplative Prayer

1. C. Luibheid, translator, *John Cassian: Conferences* (Mahwah, NJ: Paulist Press, 1985), 135-136.

2. Blofield, *The Power of the Sacred Bond*, 55.
3. J.E. Behrend, *Nada Brahma* (RoRoRo, 1949), 38.
4. R.M. French, *The Way of The Pilgrim* (New York, NY: Seabury Press), 14.
5. J.E. Behrend, *Nada Brahma*, 26.
6. Johnston, *The Cloud of Unknowing*, 8:59.
7. Ibid. 5:54.
8. Ibid. 7:55.
9. Ibid., 56.
10. Ibid. 40:100.
11. Ibid. 3:48.
12. Ibid. 25:81-2.
13. Ibid. 43:102-3.
14. Johnson, *The Book of Privy Counseling*, 2:152-3.
15. Ibid. 12:171-2.
16. Ibid. 13:172-3.
17. Johnson, *The Cloud of Unknowing*, 50:112.
18. Johnson, *The Book of Privy Counseling*, 7:162-3.
19. Walshe, *Meister Eckhart: Sermons and Treatises*, I, 4, 43.
20. Luibheid, *John Cassian: Conferences*, 39.
21. Walshe, *Meister Eckhart: Sermons and Treatises*, I, 19, 160; II, 57, 87.
22. Ibid. I, 19, 160.
23. Ibid. II, 87, 270-275.
24. Blakney, *Meister Eckhart*, "Talks of Instruction," 6, 7-10.
25. Walshe, *Meister Eckhart: Sermons and Treatises*, II, 60, 104.
26. Ibid.
27. Ibid. II, 57, 87.
28. Ibid. I, 16, 139.

29. Ibid., 13, 118.
30. Kavanaugh, *The Collected Works of St. John of the Cross*, 68.
31. Kavanaugh, *The Living Flame of Love*, 3:33.
32. Ibid., 34.
33. Ibid., 41.
34. Kavanaugh, *The Ascent of Mount Carmel*, II, 11, 11-12.
35. Ibid., 14, 2.
36. Ibid., 7, 7.
37. Ibid., 8-11.
38. Kavanaugh, *The Living Flame of Love*, 4:4
39. Ibid., 5.
40. Lucien-Marie Florent, O.C.D., "Spiritual Direction," *Carmelite Studies*, I, 1980, 7.
41. Kavanaugh, *The Living Flame of Love*, 3:60.
42. Ibid., 56.
43. Ibid., 36.
44. Ibid., 46.
45. Florent, "Spiritual Direction," *Carmelite Studies*, I, 1980, 19-20.
46. Kavanaugh, *The Ascent of Mount Carmel*, II, 22, 9.
47. Kavanaugh, *The Living Flame of Love*, 3:36.
48. Ibid., 47.
49. Ibid., 38.

Chapter 3:
The Purification Process

1. Johnston, *The Cloud of Unknowing*, 69:137.
2. Kavanaugh, *The Dark Night*, II:3:3.

3. Ibid., 10:1-2.
4. Ibid., 6:1
5. Ibid., 2,3,5,6.
6. Ibid., 16:7,8.
7. Blakney, *Meister Eckhart*, 9.
8. Walshe, *Meister Eckhart: Sermons and Treatises*: II, 87, 274.
9. Gregg, Robert C., *Athanasius: The Life of Anthony and the Letters to Marcellinus* (Mahwah, NJ: Paulist Press, 1980), 37
10. Sannella, Lee, *Kundalini: Psychosis or Transcendence?* (San Francisco, CA: H.S. Dakin Co., 1978).
11. Ibid., 59
12. Gregg, *Athanasius: The Life of Anthony and the Letters to Marcellinus*, 38.
13. Johnston, *The Cloud of Unknowing*, 49:111.
14. Ibid., 50:112.

Chapter 5:
Contemporary Considerations in Contemplation

1. Wilber, *Eye to Eye: The Quest for a New Paradigm*, 2-3.
2. Ibid., 11-12.
3. Quint, *Meister Eckhart: Deutsche Predigen und Traktate*, 353.
4. Barnstone, Willis. *The Other Bible* (San Francisco, CA: Harper SF, 1984), 302, "The Gnostic Gospel of Thomas," #22.

5. Wilber, Ken, *Up from Eden: A Transpersonal View of Human Evolution* (Boston, MA: Shambhala Publications, 1981).
6. Huxley, Aldous. *The Doors of Perception and Heaven and Hell* (San Francisco, CA: HarperCollins, 1963), 22-24.
7. Kavanaugh, *The Spiritual Canticle*, Stanzas 14-15.
8. Ibid. Stanzas 14 and 15:5.
9. Ibid., 15.
10. Ibid.

Afterword

1. Maria Shrady, Translator, *Angelus Silesius: the Cherubinic Wanderer* (Mahwah, NJ: Paulist Press, 1986), 54.
2. Kavanaugh, *The Living Flame of Love*, Stanza 4:9
3. Walshe, *Meister Eckhart: Sermons and Treatises*, I, 7, 63.
4. Ibid., 66.
5. Ibid., II, 57, 87.

About the Author

Willigis Jäger, a Benedictine monk, entered Müenster-schwarzach Abbey in Germany in 1946. After studying philosophy and theology he was ordained a priest. For several years he taught at the abbey boarding school and then worked many more years with the church groups Missio and Misereor.

Following this, Father Jäger spent six years in Japan training with Zen Master Kōun Yamada. Returning to Germany as a Zen teacher of the Sanbo Kyodan school of Zen, he opened a meditation center in Würzburg where he holds both Zen *sesshin* and courses in Christian contemplation.

Through his publications and his lectures at various congresses, Willigis Jäger has become one of Germany's best known teachers in the area of Christian and Eastern esoterics. His most recent American book is *The Way to Contemplation: Encountering God Today* (Mahwah, NJ: Paulist Press, 1987).

Library of Congress Cataloging-in-Publication Data

Jäger, Willigis.
    Contemplation: a Christian path by Willigis Jäger.
        p.   cm.
    ISBN 0-89243-690-5
    1. Contemplation.   I. Title.
    [8V5091.C7J3413 1994]
    248.3'4—dc20   94-7492
                                                        CIP